The
Rhetorical Logic
of
Henry James

The
Rhetorical Logic
of
Henry James

SHEILA TEAHAN

Louisiana State University Press

Baton Rouge and London

Designer: Melanie O'Quinn Samaha
Typeface: Bembo
Typesetter: Impressions, a division of Edwards Brothers, Inc.
Printer and binder: Thomson-Shore, Inc.

Some of the chapters in this book were first published, in somewhat different form, as follows: the Introduction as "The Rhetoric of Consciousness in Henry James," *Journal of Narrative and Life History,* III (1993), 127–37; Chapter 2 as "*What Maisie Knew* and the Improper Third Person," *Studies in American Fiction,* XXI (Autumn, 1993), 127–40; Chapter 3 as "Hawthorne, James, and the Fall of Allegory in *Roderick Hudson,*" *Henry James Review,* XII (Spring, 1991), 158–62; Chapter 5 as "The Turn of Language in *The Wings of the Dove,*" *Henry James Review,* XIV (Spring, 1993), 204–14. Permission to reprint is gratefully acknowledged.

LIBRARY OF CONGRESS CATALOGING-IN-PUBLICATION DATA

Teahan, Sheila, 1961—
    The rhetorical logic of Henry James / Sheila Teahan.
      p. cm.
    Includes bibliographical references (p.) and index.
    ISBN 0-8071-2005-7 (alk. paper)
      1. James, Henry, 1843–1916—Technique.   2. Fiction—Technique.
3. Rhetoric. 4. Logic. I. Title.
PS2127.T4T43 1995
813'.4—dc20   95-30683
                                                      CIP

For John

Contents

Acknowledgments

Although James warns us that the germination of a work is a process almost always untraceable, this project's own germination has left clear traces which are a pleasure to acknowledge. I am especially indebted to Richard Brodhead and Hillis Miller, who supported this project since its inception. Without their continuing and generous encouragement, its evolution from that original germ would not have been possible. Stephen Arch, Clint Goodson, William Johnsen, and Roger Meiners offered valuable suggestions and responses to the project as it unfolded. Chapter 5 originated in a paper in the Colloquium on Critical Theory at the University of Michigan, delivered at the kind invitation of Patricia Simpson. I am grateful to the Office of the Vice-President for Research at Michigan State, whose award of an All-University Research Initiation Grant enabled me to complete the project, and to Michele Beltran for her help in preparing the manuscript. And in the spirit of James's insistence that "art *makes* life, makes interest, makes importance," this book is affectionately dedicated to my husband, John Coogan, without whom neither the life nor the art would have been conceivable, and to Britomart, whose unsolicited emendations to the manuscript were more than compensated by her noble forbearance from eating it.

The
Rhetorical Logic
of
Henry James

Introduction

The Representational Logic of the Jamesian Center of Consciousness

Here we get exactly the high price of the novel as a literary form—its power not only, while preserving that form with closeness, to range through all the differences of the individual relation to its general subject-matter, all the varieties of outlook on life, of disposition to reflect and project, created by conditions that are never the same from man to man (or, so far as that goes, from man to woman), but positively to appear more true to its character in proportion as it strains, or tends to burst, with a latent extravagance, its mould.

—The Art of the Novel

This book investigates the rhetorical logic of Henry James's writings by means of his theory and praxis of the center of consciousness. Both a representational strategy and an implicit theory of narrative, the center of consciousness furnishes the formal principle of a large body of James's novels, as well as the focus of many of his speculative essays on writing and representation. According to this compositional law, James's reflector fictions are oriented by the perceiving consciousness of a single charac-ter—or, as in *The Golden Bowl,* a series of characters—whose putative "consciousness" or point of view is reported in third-person discourse by the text's narrator. In the critical prefaces collected as *The Art of the Novel,* James consistently associates the "germ" of individual novels with their designated centers of consciousness. As in his opening preface, where James identifies Rowland Mallet, the central intelligence of *Rod-*

erick Hudson, as the "principle of composition" that sustains the novel's formal "equilibrium," he attributes the text's very inception to the representational system of the reflective center.[1] He understands the reflector as the formal and epistemological origin and ground of his fictions, the source of structural coherence and aesthetic integrity. Further, the center of consciousness presents itself as a totalizing narrative principle not only within individual texts, but within the Jamesian corpus as a whole. James speaks of his signature compositional device as a unifying thread that runs from his first major to his last completed novel: "I should even like to give myself the pleasure of retracing from one of my productions to another . . . from 'Roderick Hudson' to 'The Golden Bowl,' that provision for interest which consists in placing advantageously, placing right in the middle of the light, the most polished of possible mirrors of the subject" (*AN,* 70).

James is fully aware of the figurative, even fictive, status of the center of consciousness, central intelligence, or reflective center, as he variously calls it. The reflective center is in fact a figure of speech that condenses two master tropes of literary representation: the mimetic trope of mirroring or reflection, and the structural metaphor of the center. It belongs to the realm of figure, not of a transparent or nonfigural critical metalanguage that would enable either James's or our own conceptual mastery of his representational practices. Moreover, indirect discourse, of which the Jamesian reflector is a technical variation, notoriously precludes any absolute rhetorical distinction between the language attributed to the central intelligence itself and the narrator's own third-person discourse. Strictly, the central intelligence cannot be extricated from the narrative it claims to organize.

James's recognition of the fundamentally rhetorical status of his central aesthetic principle would seem to circumscribe or even disable the reflective center as either representational theory or compositional strategy. Yet in *What Maisie Knew,* an exemplary center of consciousness novel, James takes as his starting point the ambiguous relation between reflector and narrator, and plays out to the full the rhetorical and causal conse-

---

1. Henry James, *The Art of the Novel,* ed. R. W. B. Lewis (1934; rpr. Boston, 1984), 15, hereinafter cited parenthetically as *AN.*

quences of this narratological ambiguity. The novel in fact turns on the impossibility of distinguishing the narrator's knowledge from Maisie's, and the linguistic blurring of this epistemological distinction brings the text to a representational impasse that culminates in "the death of [Maisie's] childhood," as the preface observes (*AN,* 146). *What Maisie Knew* thus offers a textual allegory of its own rhetorical situation. The text's ultimate abandonment of the representational intent identified in its title, that of naming Maisie's knowledge, reveals an exemplary contradiction underlying the narrative scheme described in James's retrospective preface.

Given this sophisticated level of self-reading on James's part, it comes as no surprise that his writings through and about the central consciousness are inhabited by a pervasive underthought that puts in question its explicit formal and epistemological claims. I argue that a recurring feature of the Jamesian reflector is a self-dismantling or self-negation that is staged at some point in each of the texts studied here. This dismantling takes the form of the destruction or effacement of the central consciousness itself, which is to say the character who embodies that consciousness, through a death or sacrifice enacted at the level of plot or figuration. Examples of this pattern would include Hyacinth's suicide in *The Princess Casamassima,* Milly's death in *The Wings of the Dove,* Roderick's ambiguously suicidal accident in *Roderick Hudson,* Strether's renunciatory "extinction" in *The Ambassadors,*[2] and the figurative annihilation connoted by the death of Maisie's childhood. Each of these texts culminates in the narrative and thematic sacrifice of the character who embodies its representational ground and center. In a chemical metaphor that allusively figures this sacrifice, James images the "crucible of [the novelist's] imagination" as inducing a transformative destruction of the "morsel" or experiential referent of the writer's raw material: "Its final savour has been constituted, but its prime identity destroyed—which is what was to be demonstrated" (*AN,* 230).

This sacrifice of the character in whom the reflective center is personified dramatizes the undoing or dismantling of the central consciousness as both phenomenological structure and formal device. James's nov-

2. Henry James, *The Ambassadors,* ed. Christopher Butler (1903; Oxford, 1985), 414.

els characteristically reach a narrative impasse at which the premise of
the reflective center breaks down altogether, a representational crisis variously figured or thematized as a death, sacrifice, or renunciation. This
"collapse," as James often terms the point of representational impasse, is
the collapse simultaneously of the novel's avowed representational strategy
and of its causal coherence. For the Jamesian reflector is not simply reflective or constative, as it were, but radically performative: it produces
the material it claims only to represent, causally intervening in the texts
it would organize formally. To recall the passage from *The Art of the Novel*
quoted above, it both "projects" and "reflects": the rhetorical medium
of the central consciousness is inextricable from the projection or production of plot itself. Neither a univocal theory of representation nor a
homogeneous fictional practice, the center of consciousness is a theoretical fiction or conceptual metaphor for the structures of figuration and
causality it both generates and dismantles.

    What I have characterized as the sacrifice of the Jamesian reflector is
causally linked to its fundamentally figurative status. As James acknowledges when he speaks of the narrator of *What Maisie Knew* as "trans-
lat[ing]" Maisie's consciousness into "figures that are not yet at her command" (*AN*, 145, 146), the center of consciousness effects a figurative
displacement, into third-person discourse, of the putative literal contents
of an originary first-person consciousness. But there is no accessible prior
place from which this figurative mediation departs, no available literal
term from which the narrator's metaphors are derived. The central consciousness in this sense corresponds to the trope of catachresis, a figure
for which there is no literal term. We may note that the term "figure"
itself figures centrally in James's fictional and critical writings, where it
typically carries the double meaning of number and of trope. This coimplication of the economic and rhetorical resonances of figure is critical
to James's representational system. For if the reflector is constructed by
the narrator's mediating figuration, the logic of the reflective center holds
him or her accountable for, and indebted to, those figures. The center
of consciousness pays a fatal price for the figures on which it depends.
The Jamesian expense of vision is not only a pervasive theme of James's
fiction, but an expression of the representational cost of metaphor itself.

    The center of consciousness is thus doubly indebted by this represen-

tational economy: both implicated in a figurative debt by James's characteristic economic terminology (through metaphors of payment, accountability, bankruptcy, and so on) and held accountable for the figures
in which he or she is constructed. But by its nature, this indebtedness
can never be redressed or "squared," to employ a Jamesian locution that
names the paradox at stake. Each attempt by the central consciousness to
account for itself, in either economic or narrative terms, only generates
more narrative, more indirect discourse, and therefore more figures for
which he or she is indebted in the first place. Any squaring or settling
of the narrative account contains the potential for squaring in the sense
of multiplying or amplifying the very figures that require to be squared.
In *What Maisie Knew,* the collective attempt to square Maisie by stabilizing her equivocal exchange value has the unforeseen effect of squaring
her in the sense of raising her to a higher power. But this squaring makes
her even more incommensurate or "unique," more resistant to being
squared in the sense of "worked in" or incorporated into the novel's
erotic economy. Maisie's ineluctable unaccountability is imaged as an
unpayable debt or mathematical conundrum, and her crisis of accountability at the end of the novel is figured as "an impossible sum on a
slate." [3]

Strether's correspondence with Mrs. Newsome in *The Ambassadors*
furnishes a comic version of this conundrum. Despite Strether's scru-
pulous effort to report "everything" to Mrs. Newsome, his account of
himself is shown to be in constant arrears. Each letter generates a further
proliferation of correspondence, exacerbating the problem of accountability it would resolve. The more Strether tries to account for himself,
the more there is to account for. Rather than vindicate his shift of allegiance from Woollett to Paris, his account of himself merely underlines
its intrinsic unaccountability, its resistance to rationalization or resolution
by narrative means. In what the novel terms the problem of "writing
against time," his "regular report" to Mrs. Newsome itself deprives him
of the narrative authority requisite to that reporting. [4] Strether's "regular

3. Henry James, *What Maisie Knew, In the Cage, The Pupil* (1908; rpr. New York,
1936), 360, 341, Vol. XI of *The Novels and Tales of Henry James* (New York Edition).
4. *The Ambassadors,* 182, 237; Leon Edel and Lyall H. Powers, eds., *The Complete*

report" is oxymoronic in character, for it reveals that no narrative report is regular in the etymological sense of observing a rule or law, such as the law—simultaneously asserted and denied in James's preface—that would ensure an organic development from originating germ to completed whole. Strether's report eludes the law of causality that would disclose in his actions a logical sequence of cause and effect, exposing instead the alogical erring or "deviation" discovered in James's retrospective preface (*AN*, 325).

The reflective center is held accountable especially for the disruptive effects of figuration itself, which critically intervenes in the text's causal logic. The reflector's production of the narrative events it claims only to represent thus puts in question the traditional priority of fabula and sjuzhet, or story and discourse.[5] The narratological distinction between story and discourse is, like the reflective center itself, a fiction that posits an idealist and extratextual plot, story, or idea prior to its discursive realization. In "The Art of Fiction," James avers that the distinction between the "novel of incident" and the "novel of character," between plot and characterization, is in practice untenable.[6] And though it ostensibly belongs to the realm of discourse rather than story, of sjuzhet or récit rather than fabula or histoire, the Jamesian reflector confounds the distinction between the originating germ and its discursive unfolding, since the plotting of the novels read below is as much the effect as it is the cause or given of James's compositional system. The distinction between story and discourse is elided insofar as story is produced by the very discourse of the reflective center. In particular, a recurring feature of James's fiction is the actualization of figures imputed to the central consciousness, such as the uncanny realization of Rowland's fantasy about

---

Notebooks of Henry James (New York, 1987), 556, hereinafter cited parenthetically as *Notebooks*.

5. On this distinction, see Peter Brooks, *Reading for the Plot: Design and Intention in Narrative* (New York, 1984), 12–13, 264–85, and Jonathan Culler, *The Pursuit of Signs: Semiotics, Literature, Deconstruction* (Ithaca, 1981), 169–87.

6. Henry James, *Literary Criticism: Essays on Literature, American Writers, English Writers* (New York, 1984), 55, cited hereinafter as *LC*. Subsequent references will be made to volume and page number of this text (I) and its companion volume (II), *Literary Criticism: French Writers, Other European Writers, The Prefaces to the New York Edition* (New York, 1984).

Roderick's plunge into a gulf of death and destruction in *Roderick Hudson,* or the literalization, by Hyacinth's receipt of the letter that precipitates his suicide in *The Princess Casamassima,* of the narrator's characterization of him as "an overwhelmed man of business to whom the post brought too many letters."[7] In these texts, metaphor "literally" wields the power of life and death.

This study, then, hopes to theorize the coimplication of figuration and causality in James's conceptualization and deployment of the center of consciousness. The performative effects of figure cannot be accounted for or contained by the stabilizing function of the reflective center, and this fundamental unaccountability comes to be focused on the character with whom the novel's rhetorical instability is most closely linked. Unable to account for the incalculable ramifications of figure in the text whose epistemological and metaphysical center he or she embodies, the Jamesian reflector is effaced and sacrificed in the interest of narrative closure.

As *What Maisie Knew* dramatizes, the relation between the central consciousness and the narrator who ventriloquizes it may be one of fatal ambiguity rather than benign reflection. Nor does the reflective center necessarily master the language of the narrative he ostensibly centers. In *The Princess Casamassima,* Hyacinth is not fully in control of the novel's rhetorical systems or even the particular acts of figuration imputed to him. He instead becomes the scapegoat of the subversive narrative energies released by those metaphors, which return upon him in a simultaneous displacement and containment of the revolutionary power with which the novel is thematically concerned. This "return," as the preface terms it, is both structurally and etymologically linked to the "lively inward revolution" attributed to Hyacinth (*AN,* 63, 71, 72). It points to the return or repetition of the metaphorical models through which Hyacinth perceives the novel's thematically opposed plots of art and politics. In sum, the return cryptically invoked in the preface is the turn of metaphor itself—the turnings of trope that remain beyond either Hyacinth's or James's mastery.

7. Henry James, *The Princess Casamassima* (2 vols.; 1908; rpr. New York, 1936), I, 159–60, Vols. V–VI of *The Novels and Tales of Henry James.*

The capacity of metaphor to turn beyond or away from its projected or intended path is a recurring theme of James's theoretical speculations about narrative. He defines fiction as an art of "appreciation" that entails a necessary indirection or deflection: "the affair of the painter is not the immediate, it is the reflected field of life, the realm not of application, but of *appreciation*—a truth that makes our measure of effect altogether different. My report of people's experience—my report as a 'story-teller'—is essentially my appreciation of it, and there is no 'interest' for me in what my hero, my heroine or any one else does save through that admirable process" (*AN*, 65). We may associate this appreciation with the indirect discourse through which the center of consciousness is presumptively translated or displaced. It suggests both an enlarging of value, like the increased "interest" and "value" James ascribes to his reflective centers, and a linguistic or rhetorical anamorphosis—the trope defined by J. Hillis Miller as "the transformation of one form into another which is recognizable as being a distortion of its original only when viewed from a certain angle."[8] But whereas anamorphosis assumes the existence of an original prior to this distortional transformation, the appreciation in question here affords no such access to an extralinguistic or nonfigurative original. As in the figure of catachresis, the status of a literal consciousness behind the narrator's tropological "appreciation" remains indeterminate. The center of consciousness is hypothetically transposed from first- into third-person discourse, and this discourse is itself appreciated—enlarged, translated, or otherwise anamorphostically transformed—by the narrator's putative intervening figures. Thus in *What Maisie Knew,* "Maisie's terms accordingly play their part—since her simpler conclusions quite depend on them; but our own commentary constantly attends and *amplifies*" (*AN*, 146, emphasis mine).

This tropological amplification disrupts and unsettles the representational economy it makes possible. James notes, "As soon as I begin to appreciate simplification is imperilled" (*AN*, 65): the very narrative sys-

8. J. Hillis Miller, *The Ethics of Reading* (New York, 1987), 7. On the Jamesian trope of "appreciation," see also Laurence Holland, *The Expense of Vision* (1964; rpr. Baltimore, 1982), 165, 238; and Stuart Culver, "Representing the Author: Henry James, Intellectual Property and the Work of Writing," in *Henry James: Fiction as History,* ed. Ian F. A. Bell (London, 1984), 114–36, 131–32.

tem embodied by the central reflector is destabilized by the linguistic appreciation it introduces. The restricted narrative economy of the reflector, whose formal integrity demands the narrative constraint of what James calls the "picture restricted" (*AN,* 145), cannot be reconciled with the potentially infinite linguistic appreciation it generates. It is this rhetorical excess for which the Jamesian reflector is held accountable. In *What Maisie Knew,* for example, the amplifying effects of the narrator's "figures" prove incompatible with the representational precept of the picture restricted to Maisie's consciousness. Maisie herself, who is aligned with the "residuum of truth" which James's preface enigmatically praises (*AN,* 141), comes to be figured as a residuum or remainder that must be erased if the novel's interpersonal equation is to be squared.

The figures of James's fictions thus remain beyond the mastery of the reflective centers they bring into being, and their consequences for plotting and causality are both radical and unpredictable. It is finally figurative language itself that cannot be accounted for in the Jamesian representational economy, and whose scandalous or disruptive effect is dramatized as a violent or equivocal sacrifice or renunciation. Hence my title's invocation of rhetoric's double agency, as persuasion and as figuration, inscribed in the compositional law of the center of consciousness. James's narrative system entails a systematic interference between the suasive and figurative dimensions of rhetoric: between its avowed function as organizing center and the unaccountable consequences of the figures it mobilizes, between its mimetic and performative, its reflecting and projecting, capacities.

This project, then, attempts to theorize from a rhetorical perspective the familiar Jamesian thematics of renunciation, framing it as a question of language rather than of perception, psychology, or ethics. On this view, the Jamesian topos of renunciation may be understood not merely as theme, but as rhetorical system. The ubiquitous Jamesian themes of renunciation, sacrifice, and complicity have as their linguistic counterpart a compositional law that requires the sacrifice of the character who embodies its ostensible ground. The rhetorical logic of the center of consciousness thus actualizes the "surrender and sacrifice" James identifies in *The Art of the Novel* as intrinsic to narrative art (*AN,* 6).

Other critics have ventured definitions of a Jamesian aesthetics of renunciation. In particular, readers of Laurence Holland's *The Expense of Vision* will recognize my indebtedness to his account of the thematics of complicity and sacrifice inhering in James's "sacrament of execution." Holland's study of the "sacrificial transformation of materials" wrought by James's representational aesthetic remains an authoritative statement of the ethics of Jamesian formalism. By investigating the theoretical stakes of the sacrificial thematic Holland traces, I attempt here to map the specific representational pressures of what he aptly terms "the agon *within the form.*"[9] Beyond Holland's groundbreaking lead, I have drawn upon a range of post-structuralist readings of James, either as methodological models or as points of interpretive dissent.[10]

To speak of the systematic self-dismantling of the center of consciousness is not to impute to James an artistic negligence or failed intention. The representational structure described here is a linguistic operation rather than a miscarrying of artistic intention, and James himself is always ahead of any critical formulation of it such as my own. His figuration of the novel as a genre that "tends to burst, with a latent extravagance, its mould," a tendency which James identifies as "the high price of the novel as a literary form" (*AN,* 45–46), hovers between organic and inorganic imagery, suggesting at once a containing vessel and that vessel's rupture

9.   Holland, *The Expense of Vision,* 162, 169.

10.   Particularly valuable to me has been work by Leo Bersani, Sharon Cameron, David Carroll, Deborah Esch, J. Hillis Miller, Carolyn Porter, Julie Rivkin, John Carlos Rowe, and Mark Seltzer. Several critics have linked James's thematics of renunciation and sacrifice to the problematics of representation. Geoffrey Hartman's *Beyond Formalism* offers this remarkably suggestive formulation: "James's problem is not that of facing as a writer the plenitude of things and having arbitrarily to limit it: his problem is not to be able to think of consciousness as disinterested, as a free and innocent appetite. . . . Consciousness, in other words, is not at all free or disinterested. It is knowingly or unknowingly the result of a contract, as in *Faust,* of a conspiracy, as in the Fall, or of a covenant like the crucifixion. . . . From this perspective each novel is seen to be a story that exacts from its hero and often from the storyteller himself a contractual quid pro quo. Consciousness must be paid for, and the usual wages are sacrifice and death." See *Beyond Formalism* (New Haven, 1970), 54–55. Gabriel Pearson similarly aligns Jamesian consciousness with negation in "The Novel to End All Novels: *The Golden Bowl,*" in *The Air of Reality: New Essays on Henry James,* ed. John Goode (London, 1972), 301–62. Carolyn Porter contends that Jamesian consciousness is predicated upon "a moral economy of loss"; see "Gender and Value in *The American,*" in *New Essays on "The American,"* ed. Martha Banta (Cambridge, U.K., 1987), 99–129, 124.

from within by a natural growth or fruition. Like the novel itself, the Jamesian vessel of consciousness pushes its logic, in that word's metaphysical sense of origin, end, and ground[11]—to and beyond its limit, extending its premise to the point of extravagant strain and breakage. The self-dismantling of the reflective center is in this sense the sign of its performative and positional character. (Or, strictly, of its indeterminacy in this regard; as Paul de Man warns us, to affirm the performative status of the reflector would be to return to the constative or referential category that had been put in question.[12]) The discovery or imposition of a representational ground such as the Jamesian reflective center appears to be, simultaneously, a necessity and an impossibility. In order to keep the narrative going, the novel must posit the formal and metaphysical grounding which the center of consciousness strategy offers; yet the novel's figuration must also give covert expression to the fictitiousness of this grounding.

The center of consciousness in this sense fulfills James's aspiration, announced in the preface to *The Golden Bowl,* to write in a way that demands of the writer maximum accountability: "I track my uncontrollable footsteps, right and left, after the fact, while they take their quick turn, even on stealthiest tiptoe, toward the point of view that, within the compass, will give me most instead of least to answer for" (*AN,* 328). This formulation aptly figures the problem of answerability it addresses. "Compass" here denotes range or scope, but also carries the sense of circle, circuit, circumference, enclosing line, or other boundary. Its implication of unity and closure appears incompatible with other key details: with the "uncontrollable footsteps" by which this compass is said to be reached, with the trope of turning James characteristically aligns with trope itself and its unpredictable trajectories, and finally with the passage's retrospective cast ("after the fact"), which suggests that the closure James claims to discover here is in fact an analeptic imposition. The lapses in formal continuity and causal coherence dramatized by the Jamesian reflector are, this passage affirms, a measure of its success. They attest to

11.   J. Hillis Miller, "Narrative and History," *English Literary History,* XLI (1974), 455–73.

12.   Paul de Man, *Allegories of Reading: Figural Language in Rousseau, Nietzsche, Rilke, and Proust* (New Haven, 1979).

the rigor with which James's narrative system aspires to reconcile linguistic abundance with the "sublime economy" of form, the "latent extravagance" of figuration with the confining structure of the vessel of consciousness.

The Jamesian reflector conspicuously problematizes the relation between consciousness, perception, and language—a central and recurring preoccupation of philosophy and literary theory, and one well beyond the scope of this project. Nevertheless, its specific interpretive ramifications for James's praxis may briefly be outlined. The very notion of the center of consciousness implies a phenomenology of perception, a visual model that would assimilate language to perception or "seeing," to invoke a ubiquitous Jamesian value. It is hardly surprising, then, that the Jamesian center of consciousness should have been so insistently aestheticized, in that word's etymological sense, by the critical tradition. The influential phenomenological view of James as a painterly or pictorial novelist privileges the visual representational values of ocular-centrism.[13] This critical privileging of the perceptual values of impressionism has powerful precedent in the celebrated house of fiction of the preface to *The Portrait of a Lady,* which develops a notoriously complex series of figures for the artist's task of seeing. Such, in fact, is the progressive tropological complication of James's initial positing of the million windows, each variously pierced by the "individual vision," that we are prevented from assimilating the passage's enigmatic (and perhaps not internally coherent) succession of figures to the painterly and imagistic model of representation it would seem to endorse (*AN,* 46). As Edgar Dryden, Deborah Esch, and others have recently demonstrated, this famous Jamesian endorsement of a pictorial aesthetic is pervasively qualified by his countervailing insistence on the temporal dimension of narrative, and specifically on a paradigm of textuality. As exemplary an instance of Jamesian vision as Isabel's "vigil" of "motionlessly *seeing*" (*AN,* 57) in chapter 42 of *Portrait,* a novel whose title underlines this same pictorial aesthetic, is dramatized as a series of readings that obtrude temporality into the implied spatial ideal

13.   This term is Eloise Knapp Hay's, in "Proust, James, Conrad, and Impressionism," *Style,* XXII (1988), 368–81, which provides a useful corrective to the visual orientation that inheres in accounts of James's "impressionism."

of pictorial synchrony. Contrary to the pictorial model of narrative advanced in the house of fiction passage and elsewhere, the episode reveals a systematic discontinuity between vision and language, as Dryden contends.[14] More generally, we are forcibly reminded of the irreducibly textual and graphic character of the "impression" by that word's etymological metaphor of inscription—a metaphor which James frequently plays upon, as when he speaks of the impression as a "mark made on the intelligence" (AN, 45).

Nevertheless, the formalist and phenomenological privileging of "seeing" persists in recent ideological and cultural studies of James, ranging from Carolyn Porter's Marxist critique of the Jamesian seer to Mark Seltzer's Foucauldian investigation of representational technologies of surveillance. Although the past decade of James criticism has witnessed what might be termed a shift from the phenomenology to the politics of Jamesian seeing, the prevailing visual model, with its accompanying subordination of language to perception, has for the most part been reinscribed rather than challenged. And although recent work on James has begun to address the implications of this legacy, a detailed rhetorical investigation of the center of consciousness itself has never been undertaken. The present study hopes to redress this lack by investigating the Jamesian reflective center as a rhetorical, rather than phenomenological, structure.

A related problem is posed by the persisting treatment of Jamesian consciousness, whether overtly or implicitly, as an extralinguistic category or structure. The extensive and distinguished phenomenological critical

14. Edgar Dryden, *The Form of American Romance* (Baltimore, 1988), 109–36; Deborah Esch, " 'Understanding Allegories': Reading *The Portrait of a Lady*," in *Henry James's "The Portrait of a Lady*," ed. Harold Bloom (New York, 1987), 131–53. In *The Subject in Question: The Languages of Theory and the Strategies of Fiction* (Chicago, 1982), David Carroll observes that the assimilation of language to perception in James criticism goes back at least to Percy Lubbock, who construes novelistic structure in visual and spatial terms. On the relation between language and perception in James, see especially Alexander Gelley, *Narrative Crossings: Theory and Pragmatics of Prose Fiction* (Baltimore, 1987), and John Carlos Rowe, *The Theoretical Dimensions of Henry James* (Madison, Wis., 1984), 189–252. The classic theoretical account of the problem of language and perception is to be found in Paul de Man's work on "the aesthetic ideology," notably *Blindness and Insight* (Minneapolis, 1983) and *The Resistance to Theory* (Minneapolis, 1986). For a recent study that weds the traditional perceptual orientation to the current historicizing of James, see Susan M. Griffin, *The Historical Eye: The Texture of the Visual in Late James* (Boston, 1991).

tradition on James has tended especially to take consciousness for granted in this way.[15] But the assumption of the Jamesian center of consciousness as a psychological rather than linguistic construct is equally characteristic of many sociologically oriented studies which, despite their conceptually sophisticated critique of the ideological ramifications of James's narrative practice, remain essentially wedded to a character-based approach to the novel, and so repeat the epistemological assumptions of methodologies whose ideological premises or conclusions they would be quick to contest.[16] The hypostasis of the center of consciousness as a stable and stabilizing construct, whether formal or perceptual, has remained more or less intact in much post-structuralist work on James, including Marxist, Foucauldian, psychoanalytic, and historicist treatments. With few exceptions, too, James criticism has sustained an unproblematized sense of the "center" in the center of consciousness, despite Derrida's critique of that metaphysical concept, which is conceived as simultaneously inside and outside the system it would center and control.[17] This reification and formalization of the reflective center has obscured its complexity both in the fictions themselves and in James's theoretical writings. Even among those who read James's late texts (most usually *The Sacred Fount* and *The Golden Bowl*) as questioning the epistemological authority of the reflec-

15.   Paul Armstrong's classic study *The Phenomenology of Henry James* (Chapel Hill, 1983) is among the most illuminating and theoretically advanced work in this tradition. Sharon Cameron's *Thinking in Henry James* (Chicago, 1989) develops both a critique and a rewriting of Jamesian phenomenology that challenges the phenomenological tendency to psychologize the linguistic (170).

16.   Thus Terry Eagleton assumes the organic unity of Jamesian consciousness in his charge that James's fiction "represents a desperate, devoted attempt to salvage organic significance wholly in the sealed realm of consciousness—to vanquish . . . certain real conflicts and divisions" (*Criticism and Ideology: A Study in Marxist Literary Theory* [London, 1976], 141). See also Carolyn Porter, *Seeing and Being: The Plight of the Participant Observer in Emerson, James, Adams, and Faulkner* (Middletown, Conn., 1981). Porter's account of the observer's complicity in the events he records has affinities with my own argument, though she understands this complicity in ideological (rather than rhetorical) terms, and tends to elide the distinction between "seer" and author. Mark Seltzer's Foucauldian study *Henry James and the Art of Power* (Ithaca, 1984), which investigates the continuity between "techniques of representation" and "technologies of power" (14), understands surveillance as a narratorial "seeing" that assumes the perceptual model addressed above.

17.   Jacques Derrida, "Structure, Sign and Play in the Human Discourses," *Writing and Difference*, trans. Alan Bass (Chicago, 1978), 278–93.

tor, there persists a tendency to understand James's late fiction as a critique of organicist assumptions that remain intact in his earlier fiction.

James himself contests the organicist analogy, unquestionably a pronounced feature of his critical writings, which has too often been decontextualized and taken for Jamesian aesthetic dogma. For James's ubiquitous organic metaphors of germs, grains, growth, flowering, and so on, are persistently qualified by admissions that his narratives may be, or indeed must be (though indeterminately so) incommensurate with their apparent origin or seed. In the preface to *The Ambassadors,* he marvels at "the closeness with which the whole fits again into its germ," but also acknowledges a persisting disjunction between germ and final product: "One would like, at such an hour as this, for critical license, to go into the matter of the noted inevitable deviation (from too fond an original vision) that the exquisite treachery even of the straightest execution may ever be trusted to inflict even on the most mature plan" (*AN,* 308, 325). Like Strether, who "sows his seed at the risk of too thick a crop" (*AN,* 312), James is ever at risk of uncovering a discrepancy between the originating seed and its realization. In trying the New Critical organicist view of the center of consciousness, then, I am not contesting James's overt claims to organic unity so much as drawing out their underthought in his own texts.

The arrangement of my readings of individual novels is topical rather than chronological, and I make no teleological claims about the shape of James's career. Because I take the center of consciousness to be a conceptual metaphor for certain interrelated problems of representation rather than a single or homogeneous narrative practice, my argument cuts across the traditional divisions of James's fictional praxis into such categories as the comic phase, the realist years, the scenic method, and so on. Like all such labels, these divisions tend to accrue a dubious explanatory power. James's theoretical writings must be read as critically as the novels themselves, not invoked as prescription or explanatory origin. Their insights into individual works can be yielded only through rhetorical analysis, not paraphrase or thematic extrapolation.

Yet many of James's pronouncements in *The Art of the Novel* have acquired a prescriptive and normative force, foreclosing the critical investigation they should provoke. For example, readings of *Roderick Hud-*

son traditionally echo his famous prefatory denigration of the novel's allegedly flawed time-scheme. But James's deprecating gestures of this kind nearly always mask a more oblique and complex rhetorical subtext.[18] Rather than offer a critical metalanguage or extratextual interpretive ground, the prefaces engender yet another figural text. As James asserts in "The Science of Criticism," criticism is a form of "translation" (*LC*, I, 99), a metaphorical transfer or rhetorical substitution, like the reflective center itself. On this view, his retrospective self-reading in *The Art of the Novel* appears an allegorical other-speaking, an allotropic displacement rather than a decoding of figure into concept. The discontinuities between James's theoretical formulations and his narrative praxis reveal less a disjunction *between* than a disjunction *within*. That is, both the novels and James's theoretical texts are heterogeneous in their implications for language and representation.

My thesis about the Jamesian reflector inevitably raises the question of his first-person fiction. James's habitual avoidance of first-person narration, especially in his full-length novels, is well known (*The Aspern Papers* and *The Sacred Fount* being notorious exceptions).[19] Without attempting to enforce an absolute distinction between first- and third-person narration based solely on grammatical person, I read specific narratorial interventions as significant ruptures of, or blind spots within, the compositional system of the reflector. For example, the increasing recourse to first-person narratorial intervention in the final chapters of *What Maisie Knew* signals the untenability of the claim that Maisie's knowledge exists outside the narrator's figurative "translation" of it. Such moments can be read as textual allegories in which the novels give oblique expression to their own rhetorical situation.

Since this project investigates the relation between figurative language

18.   On the figurative texture of the prefaces, see especially Cameron, *Thinking in Henry James*, 32–82 and *passim*; Carroll, *The Subject in Question*, 51–66; Holland, *The Expense of Vision*, 155–82; Rowe, *The Theoretical Dimensions of Henry James*, 219–52; and Miller, *The Ethics of Reading* and "The Figure in the Carpet," *Poetics Today*, I (1980), 107–18. On the "supplementary" character of the prefaces, see Julie Rivkin, "The Logic of Delegation in *The Ambassadors*," *PMLA*, CI (1986), 819–31.

19.   On first-person narrative in James, see William Goetz, *Henry James and the Darkest Abyss of Romance* (Baton Rouge, 1986), and Jonathan Auerbach, *The Romance of Failure: First-Person Fictions of Poe, Hawthorne and James* (New York, 1989).

and causality, the readings below are filiated as much by my interest in
the rhetoric of plot as by the topic of the central consciousness. If rhetoric
is taken in its double sense as suasion and figuration, my allied concern
is the relation between these two dimensions of narrative determination.
The Jamesian reflector is thus doubly rhetorical. As James's professed
compositional technique, it would ground and center his fictions; but
the performative effects of figure cannot be contained or accounted for
by the narrative argument of the center of consciousness. The "ironic
centre" (AN, 147), as James terms it in the preface to What Maisie Knew,
is a virtual oxymoron that names the irremediable disjunction between
the reflector's status as narrative ground and the ironic self-suspension or
self-negation[20] opened by figurative language within that grounding.

Although my emphasis in developing this argument necessarily falls
on the close reading of the novels and prefaces themselves, I also attempt
to sustain a dialogue with the growing body of New Historicist, Marxist,
feminist, and other sociological and cultural work on James. Despite
current misconceptions about the "ahistoricity," "isolationism," and "au-
totelicism" of rhetorical criticism, exemplified by recent calls for an "antiformalist" critical practice,[21] I persist in believing that rhetorical and
cultural criticism, broadly conceived, are or should be complementary
rather than antithetical. As others have argued, the critique of representation is surely an indispensable first step toward a theoretically advanced
historical or cultural criticism. And as we know from Paul de Man's
account of the profound mutual intrication of rhetoric and history, the
polarization of language or form as against history or ideology in current
critical polemics promotes a false and damaging opposition. This rhetorical study of James aspires to do justice to the historicity of his texts

20. I borrow this formulation from J. Hillis Miller, Illustration (Cambridge, Mass.,
1992), 141, who in turn alludes to de Man's work on irony in "The Rhetoric of Temporality," Blindness and Insight, 187–228.

21. Carolyn Porter's "History and Literature: 'After the New Historicism,' " New
Literary History, XXI (1990), 253–72, typifies the current demonization of formalism and
deconstruction alike, although the version of formalism Porter calls upon us to "denounce" (255) would be unrecognizable to the Russian formalists or the New Critics,
much less to readers of Derrida and de Man, whose complex critique of formalism is
ignored. Porter's celebration of "antiformalist" critical practice assumes the very seques-
tering of form from history and ideology that she wrongly imputes to so-called formalism.

as texts, for the historical fact of their nuance, complexity, and hetero-geneity as words on the page. No criticism that claims an interest in history or culture can afford to neglect this dimension of historicity. But the specific interpretive questions at stake here cannot meaningfully be addressed at the level of polemical generalization; they must be engaged at the level of close textual interpretation. I therefore consign my reflec-tion on the methodological implications of this project to my readings of the novels themselves, in the interest not of deferral, but of develop-ment—as James closes his preface to *The Portrait of a Lady,* "there is really too much to say."

I

The Politics of Metaphor in
The Princess Casamassima

Everything in the field of observation suggested this or that; everything
struck him, penetrated, stirred; he had in a word more news of life, as he
might have called it, than he knew what to do with—felt sometimes as
he could have imagined an overwhelmed man of business to whom the
post brought too many letters.

—*The Princess Casamassima*, Book I

Much like *The Princess Casamassima* itself, the story of a bookbinder fatally
torn between the conflicting demands of revolution and art, the critical
tradition on the novel is symptomatically divided between sociological
and formal concerns. Readings of the novel tend either to focus in socio-
historical fashion on the novel's political theme, or to investigate formally
its compositional device of the central consciousness, the subject of
James's influential preface. This polarization repeats the novel's own thematic opposition between politics and aesthetics—an opposition that
criticism of *The Princess Casamassima* may be compelled to repeat in one
form or another.

I want to suggest, however, that the novel's plotting and narrative
method are fundamentally and causally related.[1] Hyacinth's suicide, the

---

1. For a Foucauldian view of this relation, see Mark Seltzer, *Henry James and the Art
of Power*, which explores the "criminal continuity between the techniques of the novel
and the social technologies of power that inhere in these techniques," contending that
the strategy of the central intelligence displaces James's narrative authority onto the rev-

act that releases him from his vow to carry out an assassination for the anarchist cause, can indeed be understood not merely as a manifestation of "character" but as the consequence of his formal status as center of consciousness. Hyacinth is genetically programmed, so to speak, not only by the conundrum rhetorically encoded in his name, but by the representational premise of his role as central intelligence. For the same "bewilderment" that ensures Hyacinth's narrative value as reflector consigns him to a fatally repetitive series of linguistic errors, namely the metaphorical substitutions that confound his attempt to distinguish and reconcile the incompatible demands of art and politics. His death strictly observes the representational logic of the Jamesian reflective center, as outlined in James's preface and deployed in the novel itself. The relation between the ideological and the aesthetic in *The Princess Casamassima* is thus more vexed and complex than any binarism or thematic opposition would indicate. On one hand, the novel's political plot appears both structurally and thematically opposed to its formal strategy, since it is Hyacinth's extraordinary aesthetic sensibility as central consciousness that compromises his dedication to the anarchist cause. But on the other, the novel's revolutionary plot and its narrative method turn out to be causally intricated: Hyacinth's death follows from the very formal strategy that ensures his value as reflective center.

James's preface contends that the novel's representational law had been central to its conception and composition. Like the ideal artist in "The Art of Fiction" ("one of the people on whom nothing is lost," *LC*, I, 53), Hyacinth Robinson is "a youth on whom nothing was lost," a quintessential Jamesian observer whose susceptibility to impressions makes him an exemplary central intelligence (I, 169). Yet the novel's representational strategy rests on a paradoxical double requirement that the central consciousness be simultaneously supersensible and "bewildered." The Jamesian reflector must be intelligent enough to yield an engaging

---

olutionary leaders (57). Seltzer's alignment of omniscient narration with Foucault's panopticon implicates third-person narration *per se* in strategies of surveillance. In "Terrorism and the Realistic Novel: Henry James and *The Princess Casamassima*," *Texas Studies in Literature and Language*, XXXIV (1992), 380–402, Margaret Scanlon investigates James's unease about the novel's own questionable immunity from compromising technologies of reproduction.

"drama of . . . consciousness," yet also sufficiently "bedimmed and be-fooled and bewildered" (*AN*, 16) to produce dramatic conflict. Causality in *The Princess Casamassima* is virtually dictated by this narrative logic, which both brings Hyacinth into being and demands his ultimate sac-rifice to the rhetorical economy of the reflector. For the interpretive errors that follow from Hyacinth's capacity as an "obviously limited vessel of consciousness" (*AN*, 63) not only preclude his mastery of the anti-thetical claims of the aesthetic and the political, but condemn him to a final, fatal repetition of his own vexed and contradictory identity.

Hyacinth's plots of social ascent and artistic aspiration are figured as acts of reading and interpretation, a thematics introduced in the novel's opening passage. In a scene that literalizes James's characterization of Hyacinth as an excluded spectator of civilization and its "accumulations" (*AN*, 60), he lingers before the window of the local sweet-shop,

> an establishment where periodical literature . . . was dispensed and where song-books and pictorial sheets were attractively exhibited in the small-paned dirty window. He used to stand there for half an hour at a time and spell out the first page of the romances in the *Family Herald* and the *London Journal,* where he particularly admired the obligatory illustration in which the noble characters (they were always of the highest birth) were presented to the carnal eye. (I, 4–5)

Hyacinth attempts here to spell out his own identity, projecting himself into an imaginative world of romance much as Pinnie's "conviction that he belonged, 'by the left hand,' as she had read in a novel, to a proud and ancient race" (I, 10) casts him as hero in the archetypal romance foundling plot. His study of the emblematically titled *Family Herald* fo-cuses the novel's interrelated thematics of origins, paternity, and iden-tity—a thematics whose working out in the text is divided and contra-dictory from the start. His visit to his dying mother in prison confronts him with an origin incompatible with Pinnie's insinuations of his aris-tocratic background ("To believe in Hyacinth, for Miss Pynsent, was to believe that he *was* the son of the extremely immoral Lord Frederick," I, 11). This episode is a species of primal scene that impresses upon Hyacinth Robinson the "ineffaceable" stamp of his scandalous and contradictory origin (II, 278),[2] exposing his name as an oxymoronic crossing of plebeian and aristocrat, French and English.

Further, each component of this oxymoron is itself chiastic and contradictory. Hyacinth's mythologically resonant given name is not (as one might expect) allied with his aristocratic and romanticized father, Lord Frederick, but instead the given name of his maternal grandfather, the "republican clockmaker" who had fought on the barricades in the 1848 uprising and become "the martyr of his opinions" (I, 175). Conversely, Robinson, his father's pseudonym, is the diminutive of Robin, a traditional commoner's name, and thus associated with Hyacinth's rejected maternal heritage. (His father's real name, Purvis, perhaps a transposition of Dickens's Provis in *Great Expectations,* is derived from *purveier,* an Anglo-French verb meaning "to provide"—an ironic etymology for the name of a dissipated aristocrat who had abandoned his mistress and son.)[3] This chiastic figuring of Hyacinth's identity is repeated at multiple levels. His facility with French, viewed in Lomax Place as an aristocratic accomplishment, crosses his mother's ethnic and father's class identity. In Pinnie's eyes, his father's dissipations perversely confirm the "grandeur" of his origin (I, 11), and Hyacinth's radical sympathies are thought to reveal this same natural superiority ("These dreadful [radical] theories . . . constituted no presumption against his refined origin; they were explained rather to a certain extent by a just resentment at finding himself excluded from his proper position," I, 24–25). Like the structural oppositions around which the novel is organized (French and English, plebeian and aristocrat, art and politics), Hyacinth's name encodes an irresolvable series of crossings.

Hyacinth's paradoxical origin is also played out in the novel's intertextual allusions to its European models, especially Turgenev's *Virgin Soil.* Trilling situates *The Princess Casamassima* in the line of the nineteenth-century novel of the "young man from the provinces," the hero of mar-

---

2. On the primal scene in James, see Kaja Silverman, "Too Early/Too Late: Subjectivity and the Primal Scene in Henry James," *Novel: A Forum on Fiction,* XXI (1988), 147–73. For a psychoanalytic reading of Hyacinth's search for a maternal surrogate, see M. D. Faber, "Henry James: Revolutionary Involvement, the Princess, and the Hero," *American Imago,* XXXVII (1980), 245–77.

3. *A Dictionary of British Surnames,* ed. Percy H. Reaney (London, 1958), 262–63.

ginal origins who seeks admission to higher social circles.[4] Unlike Trilling's archetypal heroes, Hyacinth is denied the romantic or folktale transformations associated with the young man from the provinces (inheritance of fortune, dramatic social ascent). Yet the novel also rejects the Stendhalian plot of political commitment as a vehicle of self-realization. A comparison to *Virgin Soil* is instructive here: Turgenev's hero, Nezdanov, is aware of his noble birth, but the novel largely ignores his aristocratic background.[5] Although Nezdanov is, as James notes in his essay on *Virgin Soil*, "fatally fastidious and skeptical and 'aesthetic'—more essentially an aristocrat, in a word, than any of the aristocrats he has agreed to conspire against" (*LC*, II, 1003), his aristocratic birth is not posited as the source of his malaise. Nezdanov's suicide is more the result of his disenchantment with the revolutionary cause than of his conflicted identity. But rather than validate his social and intellectual ambitions, Hyacinth's aristocratic paternity simultaneously feeds his sense of social injustice, and hence his political commitment, and incapacitates him from sustaining that commitment.

This characterological double-bind is enforced by the novel's narratological premise. As James's preface explains, the ideal center of consciousness is both acutely sensitive to and wholly excluded from the intellectual world he yearns for. Only such a protagonist possesses the "*quality* of bewilderment" sufficient "not to betray, to cheapen or, as we say, give away, the value and beauty" of all that is registered by his consciousness (*AN*, 66, 67). Perversely exempted from "exclusion" from "experience of the meaner conditions, the lower manners and types, the general sordid struggle" of poverty, Hyacinth remains a "spectator" of the world he seeks to enter (*AN*, 61). In that it requires Hyacinth's simultaneous appreciation of and exclusion from "civilisation," James's nar-

4. Lionel Trilling, *The Liberal Imagination* (New York, 1953), 65–96. For an illuminating analysis of issues of paternity, legitimacy, and authority in nineteenth-century fiction that sheds considerable light on *The Princess Casamassima,* see Peter Brooks, *Reading for the Plot.*

5. Ivan Turgenev, *Virgin Soil,* trans. Constance Garnett (New York, 1920), 2 vols. On the parallels between the novels, see Oscar Cargill, *The Novels of Henry James* (New York, 1961), Lyall Powers, *Henry James and the Naturalist Movement* (East Lansing, Mich., 1971), and Taylor Stoehr, "Words and Deeds in *The Princess Casamassima,*" *English Literary History,* XXXVII (1970), 95–135.

rative technique is to this degree complicitous in his fate. If, as the narrator remarks, "nothing in life had such an interest or such a price for him as his impressions and reflexions" (I, 159), Hyacinth ultimately pays a fatal price for his status as reflective center.

This narrative logic is played out most prominently in the pervasive economic imagery common to the novel and preface. Hyacinth's origin is figured as a baffling equation or mathematical problem:

> His mother had been a daughter of the wild French people . . . but on the other side it took an English aristocrat to account for him, though a poor specimen apparently had to suffice. This, with its further implications, became Hyacinth's article of faith; the reflexion that he was a bastard involved in a remarkable manner the reflexion that he was a gentleman. He was conscious he didn't hate the image of his father as he might have been expected to do; and he supposed this was because Lord Frederick had paid so tremendous a penalty. It was in the exaction of that penalty that the moral proof for him resided; his mother wouldn't have armed herself on account of any injury less cruel than the passage of which her miserable baby was the living sign. . . . *He* was the one properly to have been sacrificed; that remark our young man often made to himself. (I, 174–75)

Here and elsewhere, Hyacinth's "disinherited" status (I, 169) is figured in the language of payment, accountability, and sacrifice. As the living sign of his mother's betrayal by Lord Frederick, Hyacinth vicariously assumes the guilt of his "recreant and sacrificed" father (I, 174) in a fantasy of compensatory martyrdom: "*He* was the one properly to have been sacrificed." The passage articulates the paradox of Hyacinth's birth in the economic terminology of accountability: "he had blood in his veins that would account for the finest sensibilities" (I, 177). This statement both reflects the seductive powers of figure and identifies a larger problem of causality in the novel. Hyacinth understands his personal qualities as proof of his paternity: only noble birth could account for his natural refinement. This reasoning assumes an identification of origin with cause, positing Hyacinth's alleged noble birth as the cause of the qualities from which it was inferred. Yet when he vows to serve Hoffendahl, the Princess cites his birth as evidence that he will "behave as a gentleman" in keeping his word; Hyacinth's aristocratic birth mandates the sense of honor that will cause him to carry out his oath (II, 250). The question of origin is governed by a double logic: Hyacinth's noble birth is posited as both cause and effect of his "fine sensibilities."[6]

This double logic is dramatized by Hyacinth's self-dedication to the revolutionary cause in chapter 21. Although he imagines that a gesture of self-sacrifice will demonstrate his "superiority" to the "raw roomful" of conspirators, a fantasy that itself contradicts his revolutionary fervor, what actually precipitates his outburst in this scene is Delancey's taunt: "There isn't a mother's son of you that'll risk his precious bones!" (I, 357, 359). Hyacinth is incited to join the cause by his identification with his disgraced mother, not by an appeal to his alleged nobility, and his involuntary outburst seems to confirm his condition as a revolutionist "*ab ovo*" (I, 342). Yet his response to Delancey's challenge is ambiguous. The syntactical framing of his actions conveys passivity, detachment, and self-spectatorship ("he found he had himself sprung up on a chair," "It appeared to him he was talking a long time," "He felt himself in a moment down almost under the feet of the other men"), and his impassioned speech to the crowd is abstract and inconclusive—he never actually offers to carry out an assassination (I, 359–60). And in the central irony of the episode, Muniment prefaces his announcement of Hyacinth's selection to meet Hoffendahl by explaining that Hoffendahl requires "a perfect little gentleman," a "lamb of sacrifice" (I, 362). Though Hyacinth is prompted to speak by an identification with his mother as representative of the London poor, he is selected as a sacrificial surrogate for the nobility on the basis of his paternal aristocratic blood.

This confusion between the anarchist and aristocratic spheres has a rhetorical counterpart in Hyacinth's own interpretive constructions as

6. My argument here is indebted to Cynthia Chase's analysis of a similar conundrum in *Daniel Deronda;* see *Decomposing Figures: Rhetorical Readings in the Romantic Tradition* (Baltimore, 1986), 157–74. In "Anarchism and Gender: James's *The Princess Casamassima* and Conrad's *The Secret Agent,*" *Henry James Review,* IX (1988), 1–16, Eileen Sypher contends that James's narrator "positions Hyacinth within an oedipal conflict that is overdetermined by a Zolaesque 'heredity' argument" (7). For a reading of Hyacinth's self-division as figuring James's own ambivalent relation to the marketplace, see Michael Anesko, *"Friction with the Market": Henry James and the Profession of Authorship* (New York, 1986), 101–18.

central intelligence. His initiation into the anarchist movement is figured in the theatrical terminology of spectacle, rehearsal, scene, and performance—the same metaphors that figure the aristocratic world Hoffendahl seeks to destroy. The anarchists and the aristocratic dilettantes are, John Carlos Rowe observes, specular doubles,[7] a specularity conveyed by the preface's oxymoronic characterization of Hyacinth as "dabbling deeply" in revolutionary politics (AN, 73). Like his revolutionary fervor, Hyacinth's social and artistic aspirations are theatrically figured:

> He was on the point of replying that he didn't care for fancy costumes, he wished to go through life in his own character; but he checked himself with the reflexion that this was exactly what he was apparently destined not to do. His own character? He was to cover that up as carefully as possible; he was to go through life in a mask, in a borrowed mantle; he was to be every day and every hour an actor. (I, 86)

Hyacinth's paradoxical concern about "keep[ing] up his character for sincerity" among the radicals (I, 341) indicates that sincerity is itself theatricalized. Poupin similarly "perform[s]" in the "character" of "political exile" while Hyacinth pledges himself to the cause and awaits word as to "the particular part he was to play" (I, 343–44). Most problematically, even Hyacinth's assassination of the duke would have been implicated in this pervasive theatricality: the Princess refers sardonically to his "famous pledge to 'act' on demand" (II, 274).

But the suicide that releases him from his pledge is equally theatricalized, as James makes clear by its ironic prolepsis in the pistol shots at the climax of "The Pearl of Paraguay." The performance literalizes this theatrical imagery and extends it to the Princess, who is introduced to Hyacinth in the "play within the play" (I, 208) enacted in her box. The episode actualizes Pinnie's early prediction that "a princess might look at you and be none the worse" (I, 157), and Hyacinth accordingly assumes that the Princess's solicitation "had something to do with his parentage on his father's side" (I, 199). Instead, her true incentive is Hyacinth's link

---

7. Rowe, *The Theoretical Dimensions of Henry James*, 171–72.

to the revolutionaries and the theatrical value of the "scenes of misery" he could disclose (I, 298): what appears an entrée to a brilliant social circle is in fact premised on Hyacinth's sociological appeal. Rather than advance his social and artistic ambitions, his intimacy with the Princess underlines his "disinherited" status, returning him to his undifferentiated infantile desire before the sweet-shop window. The Princess markedly echoes that passage: "Fancy the strange, the bitter fate: to be constituted as you're constituted, to be conscious of the capacity you must feel, and yet to look at the good things of life only through the glass of the pastry-cook's window!" (II, 60–61). Through the conflation of the sensual and aesthetic by which "the good things in life" become a child's forbidden sweetmeat, the passage diagnoses the overdetermined convergence of Hyacinth's aesthetic, social, and erotic aspirations on the Princess, the novel's metonymic focus of desire.

Hyacinth's conflicted identity is most explicitly externalized and projected in his Continental tour, the aesthetic initiation that fatally puts in question his revolutionary dedication. He suffers the imaginative excess of the overfilled Jamesian vessel of consciousness: "He had seen so much, felt so much, learnt so much, thrilled and throbbed and laughed and sighed so much during the past several days that he was conscious at last of the danger of becoming incoherent to himself and of the need of balancing his accounts" (II, 119). Recognizing Paris as "the seat of his maternal ancestors," he yet realizes that "the most brilliant city in the world was also the most bloodstained" (II, 121). This recognition actualizes the "most interesting" complication noted in James's preface, namely the irony that Hyacinth "should fall in love with the beauty of the world, actual order and all, at the moment of his most feeling and most hating the famous 'iniquity of its social arrangements' " (*AN*, 72). Martha Banta comments on the conflict between an "aesthetic" and an "ideology of history" dramatized by Hyacinth's vacillation between a willed apolitical blindness to culture's "bloody" foundations and an ideological engagement whose political goals would destroy this culture.[8] The

8. Martha Banta, "Beyond Post-Modernism: The Sense of History in *The Princess Casamassima*," *Henry James Review*, III (1982), 96–107, 100.

passage dramatizes Hyacinth's hitherto internalized division between the increasingly polarized emblematic oppositions represented by his "passionate plebeian" mother and "supercivilised" father (II, 264).

But this contradiction is no sooner exposed than resolved by Hyacinth's own figurative constructions. In a prosopopoeia that repeats his attempt "to construct some conceivable and human countenance for his father" (II, 264), Hyacinth "figure[s]" to himself his maternal grandfather, the martyred revolutionary, whom he imagines accompanying him through Paris (II, 121). Rather than enforce his revolutionary commitment, this romantic identification rationalizes the impulse to throw it over in favor of his artistic aspirations: "The feeling had not failed him with which he accepted Mr. Vetch's furtherance—the sense that since he was destined to perish in his flower he was right to make a dash at the beautiful horrible world" (II, 125). "Flower" punningly alludes to the myth of Hyacinth, and the oxymoronic conjunction of adjectives, "beautiful horrible," repeats the complicitous collusion of aesthetics and ideology, brilliance and bloodstain. If Hyacinth's scandalous contradiction of identity persists through this "transport" to "still higher sensations," this "transfer, partial if not complete of his sympathies" (II, 125), it is significant that "transport" and "transfer" name the etymological denotation of *metaphor*. The passage implies that Hyacinth's successive transfers of sympathy between an aristocratic world of leisure and the anarchist cause are groundless acts of metaphorical substitution. Thus, although he determines that book-binding "would after all translate only some of his conceptions" (II, 155), there is a sense in which his conceptions can only be translated into "translation" itself in the root meaning of a transfer or carrying over. Hyacinth's desires are radically figurative in their lack of any literal origin, goal, or referent.

His reflections on the French Revolution effect a similar figurative transfer.

He had seen in a rapid vision the guillotine in the middle, on the site of the inscrutable obelisk, and the tumbrils, with waiting victims, were stationed round the circle now made majestic by the monuments of the cities of France. The great legend of the French Revolution, a sunrise out of a sea of blood, was more real to him here than anywhere else; and, strangely, what was most present was not its turpitude and horror, but its magnificent energy, the spirit of creation that had been in it, not the spirit of destruction. (II, 140–41)

Distanced and idealized through the mediation of legend, the Revolution is seen here in both naturalizing and aestheticizing terms. The violent events evoked by the guillotine have been naturalized into an implied landscape of sea and sky, the color of blood assimilated to the crimson of an imaginary sunrise, and the entire vision invested with a "magnificent energy" that repeats the paradox of the "beautiful horrible world." Rather than renew Hyacinth's commitment to Hoffendahl, however, this vision enforces his "sense of everything that might hold one to the world." And his letter to the Princess in the same chapter, with its romanticization of Venetian poverty (II, 142–43), further dissociates him from the memory of his republican grandfather. Though he recognizes Hoffendahl's proposed revolution as a form of substitution (as he puts it to the Princess, "our friend Hoffendahl seems to me to hold [the treasures of civilization] too cheap and to wish to substitute for them something in which I can't somehow believe," II, 145), Hyacinth performs a similar substitution when he imposes an aestheticizing rhetoric on the French Revolution and then valorizes the aesthetic itself over its repressed referent.

A similar figurative resolution of ideological conflict is to be found in Hyacinth's reflections after his return from the Continent:

He had plunged into a sea of barbarism without having any civilising energy to put forth. He was aware the people were direfully wretched— more aware, it often seemed to him, than they themselves were; so frequently was he struck with their brutal insensibility, a grossness proof against the taste of better things and against any desire for them. (II, 262)

The dyslogistic rhetoric here directed against "the people" recalls the affectively charged language of James's review of *Virgin Soil*, which describes Turgenev's protagonist Nezdanov as "the 'aesthetic' young man [who], venturing to play with revolution, finds it a coarse, ugly, vulgar and moreover very cruel thing; the reality makes him deadly sick" (*LC,*

II, 1005). Yet the passage at hand insinuates Hyacinth's aestheticizing incorporation of the revolution in a quasi-apocalyptic vision:

> What was most in Hyacinth's mind was the idea, of which every pulsation of the general life of his time was a syllable, that the flood of democracy was rising over the world; that it would sweep all the traditions of the past before it; that, whatever it might fail to bring, it would at least carry in its bosom a magnificent energy; and that it might be trusted to look after its own. When this high healing uplifting tide should cover the world and float in the new era, it would be its own fault (whose else?) if want and suffering and crime should continue to be ingredients of the human lot. . . . At the same time there was joy and exultation in the thought of surrendering one's self to the wash of the wave, of being carried higher on the sun-touched crests of wild billows than one could ever be by a dry lonely effort of one's own. That vision could deepen to ecstasy. (II, 262–63)

Here the disruptive energies of social upheaval are both aestheticized for the magnificence of their destructive power and naturalized by the flood and tide imagery. And in a figurative resolution of his contradictory origin, Hyacinth is himself assimilated to the rhetoric of the passage by the sea imagery associated with his mixed parentage ("the two currents that flowed in his nature," II, 264), and thus figuratively released from the need for action through his inclusion in an impersonalized deluge of social reform. As the vaguely sexualized cast of the language suggests, moreover, the passage repeats the conflation of erotic and revolutionary energy that characterizes Hyacinth's relations with the Princess; the "surrender" and "ecstasy" of democratic fervor here envisioned are erotically charged. The passage overtly echoes his earlier hopes of induction into London's artistic circles:

> By the nature of his mind he was perpetually, almost morbidly conscious that the circle in which he lived was an infinitesimally small shallow eddy in the roaring vortex of London, and his imagination plunged again and again into the flood that whirled past it and round it, in the hope of being carried to some brighter, happier vision—the vision of societies where, in splendid rooms, with smiles and soft voices, distinguished men, with

women who were both proud and gentle, talked of art, literature and history. (I, 140–41)

Hyacinth's reflection on the Revolution duplicates the figuration of this previous fantasy. Although he appears to have exposed the mystifications of both "art" and "ideology" by this point in the novel, his epiphanic vision of universal revolution repeats the metaphors of flood and deluge that had colored his idealization of aristocratic society.

His reflections on the French Revolution conclude with yet another metaphorical transfer or reversal of sympathy. His vision of the rising "flood of democracy" conflates the metaphor of horizon with the novel's recurring light imagery, now aligned both with the Princess and with the epiphanic revolutionary vision quoted above:

> His horizon had been immensely widened, but it was filled again by the expanse that sent dim night-gleams and strange blurred reflexions and emanations into a sky without stars. . . . The Princess's quiet fireside glowed with deeper assurances, with associations of intimacy, through the dusk and the immensity. . . . Her beauty always appeared in truth to have the setting that best became it; her fairness made the element in which she lived and, among the meanest accessories, constituted a kind of splendour. (II, 266–67)

Rather than endorse Hyacinth's exaltation, the light imagery here recalls the "rosy hues" of Pinnie's complacent confidence in Hyacinth's aristocratic destiny (I, 22), the "great cold splendid northern aurora" of Hoffendahl's shadowy omniscience (II, 54), and the "aureola" of Hyacinth's own fantasy of martyrdom (II, 131). This imagery further imparts an ironic luster to Hyacinth's idealization of the Princess (Christina "Light"), equating her seductive mystifications with those of Hoffendahl. In renouncing his commitment to Hoffendahl for the artistic life that the Princess is felt to represent, Hyacinth repeats his metaphoric idealization of the conspirators; his "new convictions cast shadows that looked like the ghosts of the old" (II, 374).

In contrast to the epiphanic tone of the passages quoted above, the novel concludes with a series of negative recognition scenes marking

Hyacinth's definitive bewilderment. The fatal bewilderment of the Jamesian reflector is an ontological as well as epistemological "rupture"; as Meili Steele contends, " 'bewilderment' is James's ontological rewriting of the sublime, where the subject's categories and practices are overthrown."[9] In a literalization of James's remark in the preface that Hyacinth may "revolve round" the displays of "freedom and ease, knowledge and power, money, opportunity and satiety," but only "at the most respectful of distances and with every door of approach shut in his face" (*AN*, 60–61), he is repeatedly reduced to passive spectatorship: by his "inexpressibly representative" vision of Paul Muniment's intimacy with the Princess (II, 347); the discovery of his exclusion from Lady Aurora's "high festival . . . a scene on which his presence could only be a blot" (II, 351); Poupin's accusation that he has "ceased to believe in the people" (II, 370); and, finally, his witnessing of Millicent's self-display to Sholto as potential "purchaser" on the sexual market (II, 423). The last vignette explicitly replays the opening scene, where Hyacinth similarly gazes through a shop window at an inaccessible desired object.

Hyacinth's death inevitably follows these cancellations of his inchoate plots of erotic fulfillment and social ascent, and his final actions conspicuously repeat his crossed and contradictory origin. He recoils from assassinating the duke because to do so would be to repeat the stigmatized maternal origin he has all along labored to negate:

> He had a sense that his mind, made up as he believed, would fall to pieces again; but that sense in turn lost itself in a shudder which was already familiar—the horror of the public reappearance, in his person, of the imbrued hands of his mother. This loathing of the idea of a *repetition* had not been sharp, strangely enough, till he felt the great hard hand on his shoulder. . . . Yet now the idea of the personal stain made him horribly sick; it seemed by itself to make service impossible. (II, 419)

As Margaret Scanlon aptly observes, the performance of "The Pearl of Paraguay" enacts, in James's and Hyacinth's second language, a *répétition;* and repetition is further invoked by the Marxian allusion in Hyacinth's

9. Meili Steele, "Value and Subjectivity: The Dynamics of the Sentence in James's *The Ambassadors,*" *Comparative Literature,* XLIII (1991), 113–33, 121.

feeling that Pinnie is "turning the tragedy of his life into a monstrous farce" (I, 176).[10] The entire novel turns on the problem of repetition. For to assassinate the duke would be symbolically to repeat his mother's crime—as Trilling notes, Hyacinth is "in effect plotting the murder of his own father" as representative of the ruling class[11]—and would therefore affirm his identification with her. But by choosing the honorable alternative of suicide, Hyacinth assassinates a "duke in disguise" and an "infatuated little aristocrat," as Paul Muniment and the Princess call him (II, 217, 404), and hence figuratively *does* repeat his father's murder by destroying his father's representative in himself. His death—figuratively both a suicide and a homocide—reenacts the fates of his mother and father alike. As an attempt to escape repetition and arrest meaning, his death aspires to the closure of what Kenneth Burke has termed "an ultimate of endings, whereby the essence of a thing can be defined narratively in terms of its *fulfillment* or *fruition*." But rather than achieve the closure of a definitive identification with either parent, his death enacts "the ironic mixture of identification and dissociation that marks the function of the scapegoat"[12] in a "final" chiastic repetition of his crossed and paradoxical identity.

The novel's plotting after Hyacinth's receipt of the letter from Hoffendahl variously repeats this paradox. Hyacinth is trusted to honor his oath as a "gentleman," and is selected to assassinate the duke because he will "look in his place" at the social occasion at which the duke would be present (II, 416). Like Christopher Newman in *The American,* whose sense of honor serves as guarantee to the Bellegardes that he will never

10.　Scanlon, "Terrorism and the Realistic Novel: Henry James and *The Princess Casamassima,*" 389, 390.

11.　Trilling, *The Liberal Imagination,* 80. Millicent Bell observes that the romance foundling plot vestigially "survives in Hyacinth's recovery of his *cultural* patrimony, repeating the social conservatism of the foundling tale in his reconciliation with the paternal class" (*Meaning in Henry James* [Cambridge, Mass., 1991], 25).

12.　Kenneth Burke, *A Rhetoric of Motives* (1950; rpr. Berkeley, 1969), 13, 34. Also relevant here is Burke's discussion of "puns of logical and temporal priority" in which "source" is identified with "cause" or "essence": "the logical idea of a thing's essence can be translated into a temporal or narrative equivalent by statement in terms of the thing's source or beginnings (as feudal thinking characterized a person's individual identity in terms that identified him with his family, the paradoxical ultimate of such definition being perhaps the use of 'bastard' as epithet to describe a man's *character*)" (13).

betray their murderous secret, and thus proves only in retrospect his wor-
thiness of their daughter's hand, Hyacinth demonstrates his gentility
through a fatal renunciation. The destruction of Lord Frederick's representative in himself confirms his identification with his father. He plays
out an involuntary repetition of his "accursed origin" (I, 317), substi-
tuting himself for the duke in a figurative repetition of his mother's crime.
Thematically or conceptually, his failure to carry out the assassination is
a betrayal of the revolutionary cause. But in textual or performative
terms, Hyacinth's bid for a radical break with patterns of repetition (by
avoiding a repetition of his mother's crime, by dissociating himself from
a political movement perceived as duplicating the mystifications of the
ruling class) renders his suicide revolutionary.[13] It simultaneously breaks
and reinforces his identification with both parents, in a baffled and fatal
act of self-interpretation.

The narrator has recourse to economic terminology in accounting for
this double-edged repetition:

> He felt [the Princess] his standard of comparison, his authority, his mea-
> sure, his perpetual reference; and in taking possession of his mind to this
> extent she had completely renewed it. . . . She had in the last intimacy,
> strangest and richest of revelations, shed tears for him, and it was his
> suspicion that her secret idea was to frustrate the redemption of his vow
> to Hoffendahl, to the immeasurable body that Hoffendahl represented.
> . . . The main result of his closest commerce with her, in which somehow,
> all without herself stooping, she had only raised him higher and higher
> and absolutely highest, had been to make him feel that he was good
> enough for anything. (II, 126–27)

Here the Princess is a transcendent referent, both attesting to Hyacinth's
value and raising it to a degree that would remove him altogether from
the system of "commerce" or exchange in which he might account for
himself to Hoffendahl through a final act of self-sacrifice. Though he

---

13.   I am indebted to a discussion with Deborah White for my formulation of this
point. On the disjunction between the cognitive and performative as it relates to the
question of the promise, see Deborah Esch, "Promissory Notes: The Prescription of the
Future in *The Princess Casamassima*," *American Literary History*, I (1989), 317–38.

does not live to witness the envisioned "redistribution" which the revolution is to bring about (II, 146), Hyacinth himself becomes a token in the final settling of "the account between society and himself " (I, 36). Much as his father had "paid with his life" for the repudiation of his plebeian mistress (I, 113), so Hyacinth finally pays a "capital" penalty (II, 53) for the privilege of his aristocratic sensibilities—the antithetical "reward" for the "romantic curiosity" ascribed to Hyacinth in the preface (*AN*, 61). If his oath to serve Hoffendahl puts a "mortgage" on his life (II, 22), his suicide enacts an abrupt narrative foreclosure, a fatally peremptory settling of accounts.

The novel's narrative system indeed requires its center of consciousness to come "under the pressure of more knowledge" until his involvement with the radical cause is "out of all tune with his passion, at any cost, for life itself, the life, whatever it be, that surrounds him" (*AN*, 72–73). Even before his suicide, Hyacinth is said to be "overpast" and "extinct" (II, 418). Based as it is on his concomitant richness of sensibility and poverty of experience, the novel's compositional premise virtually demands his annihilation. Indeed, the postman's delivery to Schinkel of the fatal letter is a precise literalization of the narrator's observation that Hyacinth "had in a word more news of life, as he might have called it, than he knew what to do with—felt sometimes as he could have imagined an overwhelmed man of business to whom the post brought too many letters" (I, 159–60). There is thus a complicitous analogy between the conspirators' "direful plots" (II, 275) and James's own plotting of his protagonist's fate. Hyacinth's death observes the strict textual logic of the fatal overfilling of the Jamesian vessel of consciousness. The expulsion of the character who "know[s] too much" for "his proper fusion with the fable" (if he "knows more than is likely or natural—for *him*," the preface comments, "—it's as if he weren't at all, as if he were false and impossible," *AN*, 69) enforces an abrupt and violent closure that displaces and internalizes the novel's plotting, in both senses, into Hyacinth's "lively inward revolution" (*AN*, 72).[14] The novel's conclusion literalizes

---

14. For Rowe and Banta, the novel's conclusion symbolically displaces and recovers a social and political dilemma at the psychological or existential level of the individual psyche. Sypher reconfigures this argument in gender terms, contending that the novel subordinates the political to a domestic "failed suitor plot," invoking the female as "an

the assault of impressions recounted in the preface, the return upon Hyacinth of his extraordinary powers of sensibility: as James explains, "The interest of the attitude and the act would be the actor's imagination and vision of them, together with the nature and degree of their felt return upon him" (*AN,* 63).

This "felt return" is the return or repetition of the metaphorical models that confound Hyacinth's attempts to read and negotiate the incompatible claims of art and politics. His internal revolution is inseparable from the turnings—revolution in the etymological sense—of trope itself. *The Princess Casamassima* thematizes the dependence of the Jamesian reflector on a mediating figuration whose consequences are, like Hyacinth's suicide, unpredictable and potentially revolutionary. For this reason, the novel implicitly endorses the concept of an "economy of heroism"—the philosophy, rejected by Poupin at the conspirators' meeting, that two men should never be sacrificed for the cause "where one will serve" (I, 351, 352): Hyacinth both functions as scapegoat for a generalized political target and serves the narrative economy of the reflective center. The novel contains Hyacinth's antithetically "aggressive, vindictive, destructive social faith" (*AN,* 72) by redirecting against him an act of revolutionary violence. Its allusion to the myth of Hyacinth may gesture toward a redemptive mythic subtext, though this subtext would inevitably repeat the myth's own bifurcated ambiguity, dramatized in its conflicting versions, as to whether the death of Hyacinthus is generically comic or tragic, the result of accident or of Zephyr's murderous jealousy.[15]

James's narrator withdraws altogether from Hyacinth's "consciousness" in the final chapters. Like the contents of the letter from Hoffendahl containing his orders, his unrepresented crisis of conscience remains an indeterminate blank. The novel's compositional system elides this ethical crux, forbidding us to read the conclusion in psychological or other

---

'Other,' as a vehicle for collecting otherwise unmanageable fears and desires" ("Anarchism and Gender: James's *The Princess Casamassima* and Conrad's *The Secret Agent,*" 7, 2).

15. In Ovid, Hyacinth's death occurs accidentally during a discus contest with Apollo. In other versions of the myth, however, Zephyr blows Apollo's discus toward Hyacinth in an act of jealousy. See Reid Badgers, "The Character and Myth of Hyacinth: A Key to *The Princess Casamassima,*" *Arizona Quarterly,* XXXII (1976), 316–26.

naturalizing terms. Though the Jamesian center of consciousness may appear the ultimate vehicle of psychological realism, it finally dismantles its central assumptions, such as the idea of narrative as a mimetic presentation of consciousness. Hyacinth's fate seems a function primarily not of ethical, psychological, or political forces but of the rhetorical logic of the central intelligence itself, and of the play of figure on which that logic depends. Despite its reputation as a masterpiece of James's "social realist" phase, *The Princess Casamassima* hollows out the conventions of social realism with thoroughgoing irony. In *What Maisie Knew,* a novel traditionally identified as a masterpiece of Jamesian psychological realism, this irony is formalized into the compositional principle of the ironic center of consciousness—though in a manner that ironically challenges the very foundations of James's narrative system.

2

What Maisie Knew and the Improper Third Person

Has a *part* of all this wasted passion and squandered time (of the last 5 years) been simply the precious lesson, taught me in that roundabout and devious, that cruelly expensive, way, *of the singular value for a narrative plan too* of the (I don't know *what* adequately to call it) divine principle of the Scenario? If that *has* been one side of the moral of the whole unspeakable, the whole tragic experience, I almost bless the pangs and the pains and the miseries of it. IF there has lurked in the central core of it this exquisite truth—I almost hold my breath with suspense as I try to formulate it; so much, so *much,* hangs radiantly there as depending on it—this exquisite truth that what I call the divine principle in question is a key that, working in the same *general* way fits the complicated chambers of *both* the dramatic and the narrative lock: IF, I say, I have crept round through long apparent barrenness, through suffering and sadness intolerable, to that rare perception—why my infinite little loss is converted into an almost infinite little gain.

—*Notebooks*

What Maisie Knew's psychologically and linguistically involuted exploration of adultery from a child's perspective appears claustrophobic beside the Dickensian scope and texture of *The Princess Casamassima.* Yet James's preface to *Maisie* emphasizes the novels' affinities. Like Hyacinth, who "collapses . . . like a thief at night, overcharged with treasures of reflexion and spoils of passion of which he can give, in his poverty and obscurity, no honest account" (*AN,* 156), Maisie is remarkable for "the weight of the tax" on her case (*AN*, 150), valuable for her very resistance to the pressure exerted by James's compositional law. Yet the novels' formal affiliation extends to a much deeper exploration of the epistemology of figure in Jamesian narrative. For its investigation of the connections between metaphor and the knowledge it enables, *What Maisie Knew* is the exemplary Jamesian center of consciousness novel.

James's preface conveys an unease about the novel's theme, a young girl surrounded by the adulterous intrigues of her parents and stepparents, and he defensively anticipates charges of having "mixed Maisie up" in the novel's erotic quadrangle. As often in the history of James criticism, the preface has proved a self-fulfilling prophecy: critics have typically repeated the antinomies of James's own ambivalence, replaying the novel's internal debate as to whether Maisie is innocent or corrupt, ingenuous or precociously wise—replaying, in short, the ambiguity about how much Maisie knows.[1] James and his critics are not mistaken in their intuition that Maisie's equivocal knowledge invites the kind of investigation thematized by Mrs. Wix's probings of her "moral sense." But the critical doubts about the moral sense of *What Maisie Knew* may respond less to its adulterous plot than to a representational strategy that creates the stigmatized knowledge it professes to reflect: for although the narrator claims merely to report Maisie's knowledge, he is in fact deeply implicated in its construction.

As its title indicates, *What Maisie Knew* is overtly concerned with the epistemology of the Jamesian reflector. The "delightful difficulty" (*AN*, 144) of the novel's strategy is its restriction of perspective to Maisie's impressions; as James's notebook entries affirm, "Make my point of view, my *line*, the consciousness, the dim, sweet, sacred, wondering, clinging perception of the child . . . EVERYTHING TAKES PLACE BEFORE MAISIE. That is a part of the essence of the thing" (*Notebooks*, 148, 149). But because "[s]mall children have many more perceptions than they have terms to translate them," this strategy posits a rhetorical disjunction between narrator and vessel of consciousness. If Maisie is an "infant" (*AN*, 145) in the etymological sense of *infans*, speechless or without language, then the

---

1.   For the classic instance, see the Leavis-Bewley exchange in *The Complex Fate* (London, 1952).

"great gaps and voids" of her linguistic resources must be filled by the
narrator himself. Thus, although "Maisie's terms accordingly play their
part," the narrator's "own commentary constantly attends and amplifies,"
translating Maisie's perceptions into "figures that are not yet at her command" (*AN,* 146). He amplifies or enlarges Maisie's terms, providing
figures for the inaccessible literal terms of her consciousness, and so fills
out the lacunae of her verbal resources. His compositional strategy resembles what narratology terms dissonant psycho-narration, the narrative
representation of preverbal subjectivity in language other than the character's own (as distinct from consonant psycho-narration, which represents subjectivity through imitation, for example by mimicry of the character's diction or syntax).[2]

This scheme may account for the defensive tone of the preface.[3] James
justifies the selection of a female vessel of consciousness on the grounds
that "the sensibility of the female young is indubitably, for early youth,
the greater": by casting "a slip of a girl" as his reflector, he secures for
his story " 'no end' of sensibility" (*AN,* 143–44). But in his eagerness to
forestall the objection that "nothing could well be more disgusting than
to attribute to Maisie so intimate an 'acquaintance' with the gross im-
moralities surrounding her" (*AN,* 149), James acknowledges the epistemological conundrum pointed to by the novel's title. For given the impossibility of distinguishing the narrator's terms from Maisie's, since she
can know only what the narrator tells us she knows, "what Maisie knew"
designates a symbiotic and asymmetrical narrative relation in which her
knowledge depends on its articulation by the narrator. And despite
James's readiness to discount the charge of " 'mixing-up' . . . a child with
anything unpleasant," it is precisely Maisie's status as "extraordinary
'ironic centre' " of the novel's adulterous "connexions" that assures her
"highest exhibitional virtue" and produces her "all but incalculable" effect (*AN,* 148–49, 147).

The evolution of this scheme may be traced in James's notebook en-

---

2. On this distinction, see Steven Cohan and Linda M. Shires, *Telling Stories: A
Theoretical Analysis of Narrative Fiction* (New York, 1988), 100.

3. As Neil Hertz has noted, James's unease invites comparison to Freud's defensive-
ness in *Dora;* see "Dora's Secrets, Freud's Techniques," *The End of the Line* (New York,
1985), 122–43.

tries. He first contemplates a plot in which the death of Maisie's parents would cause her to be "divided" by her stepparents, but concludes that "the very essence of the subject" requires that the divorced parents live, speculating that the "most *ironic* effect" would be achieved "if I make the old parents, the original parents, *live,* not die, and transmit the little girl to the persons they each have married *en secondes noces*" (*Notebooks,* 147, 148, 77). If one of the parents dies, "the situation breaks" (*Notebooks,* 77): for the sake of the "proper symmetry" that would permit "the case to begin, at least, to stand beautifully on its feet" (*AN,* 140, 142), the novel's formula requires the remarriage of each parent. Accordingly, the novel opens with a divorce settlement in which Maisie is "divided in two and the portions tossed impartially to the disputants" (4). The parents' names are ironically resonant: Ida recalls the nymph who protected the infant Zeus from being devoured by his father Cronus—an apt analogue for the fate of a child who is divided and tossed to rapacious parents. "Beale Farange," who first appears in the notebooks as the more bluntly allegorical "Hurter," punningly suggests "far-range bale." This pun indeed resonates with the numismatic metaphor in James's preface that compares Maisie's equivocal effect to the anomaly of a coin with two antithetical faces: "No themes are so human as those that reflect for us, out of the confusion of life, the close connexion of bliss and bale, of the things that help with the things that hurt, so dangling before us for ever that bright hard metal, of so strange an alloy, one face of which is somebody's right and ease and the other somebody's pain and wrong" (*AN,* 143). In the manner of this strange alloy, Maisie operates as a two-faced coin that signifies both bliss and bale, right and wrong. Her effect is anomalous and alogical, like a coin stamped with two incompatible values. James's formulation, which concludes with a chiastic reversal of the final doublet ("pain and wrong" rather than the expected "wrong and pain"), is itself chiastic or asymmetrical, a tiny figure for the novel's larger chiastic structure.

Despite James's denial of having mixed Maisie up in adulterous alignments, the novel's opening figuratively repeats exactly this crime: "The evil [Maisie's parents] had the gift of thinking or pretending to think of each other they poured into her little gravely-gazing soul as into a boundless receptacle" (14). The novel's "light vessel of consciousness" (*AN,*

143) becomes "a ready vessel for bitterness, a deep little porcelain cup in which biting acids could be mixed" (5), aligning Maisie's compositional function as center of consciousness with her role as receptacle for her parents' bitterness. The cup and vessel imagery associated with the Jamesian reflector is pointedly linked to the disjunction between the narrator's figures and Maisie's own verbal capacity.

> By the time she had grown sharper, as the gentlemen who had criticized her calves used to say, she found in her mind a collection of images and echoes to which meanings were attachable—images and echoes kept for her in the childish dusk, the dim closet, the high drawers, like games she wasn't yet big enough to play. The great strain meanwhile was that of carrying by the right end the things her father said about her mother— things mostly indeed that Moddle, on a glimpse of them, as if they had been complicated toys or difficult books, took out of her hands and put away in the closet. A wonderful assortment of objects of this kind she was to discover there later, all tumbled up too with the things, shuffled into the same receptacle, that her mother had said about her father. (12)

This passage covertly addresses the novel's central concern with the relation between language and knowledge. Like the unconscious, the Jamesian receptive intelligence becomes the repository of the internalized objects of knowledge (and especially forbidden sexual knowledge), linked by the toy analogy to the game imagery by which the novel designates adulterous liaisons.[4] It is notable that Moddle stands in for the force of repression that consigns the forbidden toys to the ostensibly preverbal unconscious. As the novel's epitome of linguistic muddlement (James writes in the preface, "The effort really to see and really to represent is no idle business in face of the *constant* force that makes for muddlement," *AN,* 149), a comic character identified with Maisie's own "distressful lapses in the alphabet" (16), Moddle parodically doubles Maisie's verbal incompetence and so embodies the ultimate "muddled state" (*AN,* 149).

Yet Maisie's dilemma in this particular passage is not her verbal incapacity, but her inability to interpret what she hears. The passage reverses

4. On this imagery, see Juliet Mitchell, "*What Maisie Knew:* Portrait of the Artist as a Young Girl," in *The Air of Reality: New Essays on Henry James,* ed. Goode, 168–89.

and corrects, so to speak, the theory of language latent in the preface, proposing instead that Maisie's terms produce, rather than represent or translate, her thought. These possibilities correspond, respectively, to performative and constative theories of language: the question is whether, in giving terms to Maisie's knowledge, James's narrator merely expresses an existing preverbal consciousness or actually creates it. By acknowledging the ambiguity of the narrative premise that posits Maisie's linguistic dependence on the narrator, the passage calls attention to what, following Neil Hertz's characterization of Freud's relation to Dora, one might call the "epistemological promiscuity" that confounds the distinction between the narrator's knowledge and Maisie's.[5] James's representational strategy thus repeats the very crime of adulteration attributed to Maisie's parents—an adulteration compounded by his retrospective insistence that "my light vessel of consciousness, swaying in such a draught, couldn't be with verisimilitude a rude little boy" (*AN*, 143). For as the narrator remarks of the unsuitability of appointing Sir Claude as her guardian, "The essence of the question was that a girl wasn't a boy" (302): Maisie's gender facilitates her implication in erotic intrigue, notably her competition with Mrs. Beale and Mrs. Wix over Sir Claude late in the novel. *What Maisie Knew* oddly activates the sexualized cast, elsewhere latent, of the Jamesian "penetrating imagination" (*AN*, 78).

But in a reversion to the theory of language posited in the preface, the narrator goes on to assert that Maisie's internalized images will be delivered to her verbalized consciousness when her linguistic ability catches up with her perceptions.

> She was at the age for which all stories are true and all conceptions are stories. The actual was the absolute, the present alone was vivid. The

---

5. Hertz, *The End of the Line*, 136. For other views of Maisie's relation to the narrator, see Merla Wolk, "Narration and Nurture in *What Maisie Knew*," *Henry James Review*, IV (1983), 196–206; Sallie Sears, *The Negative Imagination: Form and Perspective in the Novels of Henry James* (1963; rpr. Ithaca, 1968), 22–34; Bell, *Meaning in Henry James*, 243–61; and Julie Rivkin, "Resisting Readers and Reading Effects: Some Speculations on Reading and Gender," in *Narrative Poetics: Innovations, Limits, Challenges*, ed. James Phelan (Columbus, Ohio, 1987), 11–22. Rivkin associates the "resistance" ascribed to Maisie in James's preface with her potential resistance to, and ironic distance from, the reading imposed by the narrator's translation of her experience.

objurgation for instance launched in the carriage by her mother after she had at her father's bidding punctually performed was a missive that dropped into her memory with the dry rattle of a letter falling into a pillar-box. Like the letter it was, as part of the contents of a well-stuffed post-bag, delivered in due course at the right address. (14)

Reminiscent of Hyacinth's condition as the man to whom the post brought too many letters, the passage projects an eventual delivery from the receptacle of memory, an "overflowing" (14) that threatens to overwhelm Maisie's receptive consciousness. If, like a metaphor, a translation is a species of transfer that never quite delivers (one thinks of Maisie's letters from her mother, which are consistently intercepted by Miss Overmore), the passage does not spell out the implications of such a delivery. When will this delivery take place? At what point, that is, does Maisie "know"?

Maisie's unwitting mediation between her parents as "faithful reporter" is ironically repeated when she inadvertently brings her father and Miss Overmore together.

> The theory of her stupidity, eventually embraced by her parents, corresponded with a great date in her small still life: the complete vision, private but final, of the strange office she filled. It was literally a moral revolution and accomplished in the depths of her nature. . . . She puzzled out with imperfect signs, but with a prodigious spirit, that she had been a centre of hatred and a messenger of insult, and that everything was bad because she had been employed to make it so. . . . She saw more and more; she saw too much. It was Miss Overmore, her first governess, who on a momentous occasion had sown the seeds of secrecy; sown them not by anything she said, but by a mere roll of those fine eyes which Maisie had already admired. (15–16)

Overmore herself seems an extension by wordplay of the key terms of the passage ("overflowings," "more and more"), as if she were the product of Maisie's verbal imagination. Like the excess or superfluity her name signifies, Overmore destabilizes the novel's interpersonal economy by introducing a new element to the novel's "personal equation," as James calls the intersubjective plot of the English novel (*AN*, 184). She thus initiates the novel's "wild game of 'going round' " (18), the adulterous realignments and "distribution of parties," "a rushing to and fro and a changing of places" (95). Like Maisie, Overmore embodies a paradoxical compound of simultaneous excess and lack, as reflected in James's notebook experimentations with her name: "Overmore–Undermore–Overend" (*Notebooks*, 140). In an equivocal analogue of Maisie's own redemptive activity, imputed to her in the preface, of "sowing on barren strands, through the mere fact of presence, the seed of the moral life" (*AN*, 143), Miss Overmore here sows the seeds of Maisie's "secrecy"— her refusal to repeat her parents' mutual accusations. Yet because it is readable as compromising knowledge, Maisie's silence fosters the contradictory impressions of "extreme cunning or . . . extreme stupidity" (15), like the "excess of the queer something which had seemed to waver so widely between innocence and guilt" from which her lack of a moral sense is finally inferred (232).

In her capacity as "a centre and pretext for a fresh system of misbehaviour" (*AN*, 143), Maisie in fact creates the domestic scandal she is initially thought to condemn. She keeps Beale and Miss Overmore "perfectly proper," providing them with a *locus standi* or "leg to stand on before the law" and so permits James's narrative itself to "stand beautifully on its feet" (39, 36; *AN*, 142). She creates "fresh tie[s]" (*AN*, 142) and forges "an extraordinary link between a succession of people" (*Notebooks*, 147), bringing together her stepparents and supplying them with a "jolly good pretext" (189) such that they become "interested and attached, finally passionately so" (*Notebooks*, 71). Ida's accusing glare at her daughter "as at an equal plotter of sin" (143) underlines Maisie's authorial power as unwitting architect of the novel's adulterous intrigues. Though passive "subject of the manoeuvres of a quartette" (198), she is ironically complicitous in the plot that evolves from her compositional function as reflector.

Maisie's duality as author and victim of the novel's adulterous plot is reflected in its central patterns of figuration. The preface refers to her "terribly mixed little world," and James's sensitivity to "the 'mixing-up' of a child with anything unpleasant" is doubled by Sir Claude's concern about "mix[ing Maisie] up" in his own liaison (*AN*, 143, 148–49; *WMK*, 167). Yet this crime is replicated in Maisie's "poison[ing]" or adulteration at the levels of plot and representational strategy alike (89). By furnishing his vessel of consciousness with the terms of forbidden knowledge, the narrator mixes her up or adulterates her, tampering with her initially unadulterated purity and so producing the equivocal coin of James's preface, "that bright hard metal, of so strange an alloy, one face of which is somebody's right and ease and the other somebody's pain and wrong." The novel plays throughout on the multiple meanings of "adulterate": to commit adultery (obsolete, *OED* 1); to debauch or defile by adultery (obsolete, *OED* 2); to render spurious or counterfeit, falsify or corrupt, or debase by the admixture of baser ingredients (*OED* 3).

The text seems uncertain about where responsibility for this dilemma should be assigned; in both the novel and preface, the culpability for Maisie's contamination shifts repeatedly between the narrator, the other characters, and Maisie herself. For if Maisie sows on barren strands the seed of the moral life, she equally "spread[s] and contagiously act[s]": the foundational germ of James's narrative is both life-giving seed and agent of disease, a "virus of suggestion" (*AN*, 148, 119). Even while "keeping the torch of virtue alive in an air tending infinitely to smother it," in a figure that resonates with the "torch of rapture and victory" aligned in the preface with James's own authorial imagination, Maisie contagiously acts upon the "infected air" in which she equivocally "flourish[es]" (*AN*, 143, 141, 149). Her contagious activity appears continuous with the infected air over which she triumphs; she is both hygienic and pestilential.

This duality may be seen, too, in the novel's pervasive linear imagery. To borrow J. Hillis Miller's coinage, Maisie is an "Ariachne" who collapses and conflates the myths of Ariadne and Arachne. The myth of Ariadne illustrates the relation between linear imagery and the problem of repetition in narrative, whose logic dictates that "[t]he line of Ariadne's thread is at once the means of retracing a labyrinth which is already there, and at the same time is itself the labyrinth . . . spun from the belly of a spider in mid-web, Ariadne anamorphosed into Arachne."[6] With her "small smug conviction that in the domestic labyrinth she always kept the clue" (90), Maisie is an Ariadne figure who possesses the thread of

6. J. Hillis Miller, "Ariadne's Thread: Repetition and the Narrative Line," *Critical Inquiry,* III (1976), 57–77, 67.

escape from the novel's labyrinth of adulterous intrigue, the antidote to its "infected air." But, as the preface tells us, she also "weav[es] about, with the best faith in the world, the close web of sophistication" (*AN*, 143), spinning a new network of interpersonal entanglement, a web of sophistication in the double sense of corruption or adulteration and of the verbal proficiency made possible by the narrator's linguistic mediation. Both Arachne and Ariadne, spinner of the labyrinthine web of adultery and the means of escape from it, Maisie weaves and unweaves the novel's "displayed tangle of human relations" (*AN*, 63). Spiderlike, she "embalms" everything she reflects as central intelligence ("she treats her friends to the rich little spectacle of objects embalmed in her wonder," *AN*, 146), entangling yet preserving the objects presented to her consciousness. She creates "complications" in the etymological sense of folds or weavings; James's notebook refers to her charm, "so complicating and entangling for others" (*Notebooks*, 166).

Even James finds himself entangled in the resulting narrative web: his preface indeed figures writing as the straightening of a tangle, a "pulling at threads intrinsically worth it" (*AN*, 146). In her capacity as "centre and pretext for a fresh system of misbehaviour, a system moreover of a nature to spread and ramify," Maisie develops the narrative design imaged as a tree in the opening figure of James's preface: "I recognize again, for the first of these three Tales, another instance of the growth of the 'great oak' from the little acorn; since 'What Maisie Knew' is at least a tree that spreads beyond any provision its small germ might on a first handling have appeared likely to make for it" (*AN*, 140). This trope is actualized by the tree beneath which Maisie sits with the Captain in chapter 16, a "spreading tree" (*AN*, 149) verbally aligned with the novel's own ramifying narrative. (In an ironic duplication of the narrator's activity of translation, Maisie appears in this scene to censor the expletive Sir Claude hurls at his wife: "You damned old b——!" When questioned later by the Captain, Maisie reports, "He has called her a damned old brute," 145, 146.) Like the text itself, the web of Maisie's "spreading and contagious action" creates a configuration whose narrative ramifications are incommensurate with their foundational germ, neither foreseen nor accounted for by their ostensible origin in Maisie's perceiving consciousness.

For the narrator, the characters, and James himself, Maisie's uncanny ability to generate plot developments eludes logical explanation. Thematically, this puzzle is expressed as the question of Maisie's moral sense; tropologically, it is figured as a debt she incurs. The novel figures this indebtedness in Maisie's educational deficit: she has "such a tremendous lot to make up" (82) as a result of missed lessons during her stay with her father and his new wife. When she returns to her mother, "the idea of what she was to make up and the prodigious total it came to were kept well before Maisie," like the sum of a debt. In compensation for this lack, Mrs. Wix institutes a rigorous lesson plan, and "The year . . . rounded itself as a receptacle of retarded knowledge—a cup brimming over with the sense that now at least she was learning" (66). This image plays on the familiar trope of the Jamesian reflector as receptacle, but also suggests the equivocal character of Maisie's knowledge—a faintly oxymoronic retarded knowledge of simultaneous belatedness and precocity, lack and overflow. Like the two-faced coin of the preface, Maisie circulates in this economy as double-edged currency, simultaneously redemptive and destructive.

That Maisie herself is to be held accountable for the settling of the novel's personal equation becomes clear after the chiastic plot structure that brings together Miss Overmore (now Mrs. Beale) and Sir Claude. The episode in question hinges on the realization that "no one after all had been squared," and concludes with an ironic revelation, Maisie's

> dim apprehension of the unuttered and the unknown. The relation between her step-parents had then a mysterious residuum; this was the first time she really had reflected that except as regards herself it was not a relationship. (168)

This residuum is an unaccountable remainder, as of an unbalanced equation or chemical analysis. It is recalled in the "residuum of truth" identified in James's retrospective preface with the "ironic truth" Maisie is said to produce as center of consciousness (AN, 141, 142). The alliance between Claude and Mrs. Beale, in which Maisie is instrumental, leaves a mysterious residue or residuum of fundamental unaccountability.[7]

7. A Lacanian reading of this "residuum" is to be found in Dennis Foster, "Maisie Supposed to Know: Amo(u)ral Analysis," *Henry James Review,* V (1984), 207–16.

This chemical troping is pervasive in James's theoretical writings. *The Art of the Novel* figures representation as a process of chemical analysis and reduction, an "exquisite chemistry" of foreshortening or "rare alchemy" by which the "crucible" of the novelistic imagination reduces its subjects to their essences (*AN*, 87, 230). At stake in the chemical imagery in *What Maisie Knew* is the novel's narrative metaphysics. Maisie's equivocal agency is figured by the economic and chemical terminology that tropes her as a mathematical remainder or chemical residuum that must be erased if the text's narrative economy is to be satisfactorily squared.[8] According to this figurative logic, everyone would be squared if Maisie could be made to understand these figures, in the dual sense of number and of trope. But the attempt to redress the lack in Maisie's education only implicates her further in the compromising knowledge against which it would inoculate her.

> The institution—there was a splendid one in a part of the town but little known to the child—became, in the glow of such a spirit, a thrilling place, and the walk to it from the station through Glower Street (a pronunciation for which Mrs. Beale once laughed at her little friend) a pathway literally strewn with "subjects." Maisie imagined herself to pluck them as she went, though they thickened in the great grey rooms where the fountain of knowledge, in the form usually of a high voice that she took at first to be angry, plashed in the stillness of rows of faces thrust out like empty jugs. (164)

The jugs offer a droll literalization of the Jamesian vessel of consciousness, and the fountain image plays ironically on the "danger of filling too full any supposed and above all any obviously limited vessel of consciousness" (*AN*, 63) intrinsic to the reflector strategy. Yet what would qualify as filling too full the vessel of Maisie's consciousness? The tenor of James's figure is unclear. The sexualized imagery of the preface vaguely eroticizes the relation between vessel of consciousness and the authorial penetrating imagination. And the plot ultimately turns on the question of Maisie's own emergent sexuality, of her increasing instrumentality in its adulterous "violent substitution[s]" (301). Despite Claude's attempts to desexualize

---

8. On the trope of "squaring" in the novel, see Barbara Eckstein, "Unsquaring the Squared Route of *What Maisie Knew*," *Henry James Review*, IX (1988), 177–87.

her by addressing her as "old chap," "Maisie boy," and so on (332, 262), she is unmistakably implicated in the novel's interlocking erotic triangles. Like James's, Sir Claude's relation to Maisie is simultaneously paternal and sexualized; his early gift to her of a "Moonlight Berceuse" (135), a moonlight cradle song or lullaby imbued with romantic connotations, exemplifies this ambivalence.

The overfilling of Maisie's vessel of consciousness calls into question the text's foundational rhetorical strategy, which assumes that her knowledge exists prior to the narrator's figurative translation of it.

> Maisie had known all along a great deal, but never so much as she was to know from this moment on and as she learned in particular during the couple of days that she was to hang in the air, as it were, over the sea which represented in breezy blueness and with a summer charm a crossing of more spaces than the Channel. It was granted her at this time to arrive at divinations so ample that I shall have no room for the goal if I attempt to trace the stages; as to which therefore I must be content to say that the fullest expression we may give to Sir Claude's conduct is a poor and pale copy of the picture it presented to his young friend. Abruptly, that morning, he had yielded to the action of the idea pumped into him for weeks by Mrs. Wix on lines of approach that she had been capable of the extraordinary art of preserving from entanglement in the fine network of his relations with Mrs. Beale. (202–203)

The narrator's attempted representation of Maisie's knowledge yields only a poor copy of a picture, a doubly refracted diegesis that relegates it to a triple displacement from Maisie's consciousness. The novel's presumptive strategy of "the picture restricted" (*AN*, 145), sustained indirect discourse limited to Maisie's perspective, is in danger of collapse. The chapter proceeds by a series of disclaimers of the narrator's authority to represent what Maisie knew:

> It sounds, no doubt, too penetrating, but it was not all as an effect of Sir Claude's betrayals that Maisie was able to piece together the beauty of the special influence through which, for such stretches of time, he had refined upon propriety by keeping, so far as possible, his sentimental interests distinct. She had ever of course in her mind fewer names than conceptions . . . (204)

I may not even answer for it that Maisie was not aware of how, in this, Mrs. Beale failed to share his all but insurmountable distaste for their allowing their little charge to breathe the air of their gross irregularity . . . Their little charge, for herself, had long ago adopted the view that even Mrs. Wix had at one time not thought prohibitively coarse—the view that she was after all, *as* a little charge, morally at home in atmospheres it would be appalling to analyse. (205)

Oh decidedly I shall never get you to believe the number of things she saw and the number of secrets she discovered! Why in the world, for instance, couldn't Sir Claude have kept it from her—except on the hypothesis of his not caring to—that, when you came to look at it and so far as it was a question of vested interests, he had quite as much right in her as her stepmother, not to say a right that Mrs. Beale was in no position to dispute? (205–206)

As signaled by its modulation into the second person, this last passage finally veers into Claude's own idiomatic inflection. But its chief strategy is a paralepsis that veils over Maisie's knowledge in the guise of revealing it; unable to say what Maisie knows, the narrator is reduced to claiming that it resists representation altogether.

All the narrator *can* articulate, in fact, is his inability to answer for Maisie's knowledge and its uncanny effects. The above passage explicitly worries over the central vulnerability of James's narratorial premise, namely the claim that her knowledge is extralinguistic: "She had ever of course in her mind fewer names than conceptions" (204). But the narrator's introductory apologia ("It sounds, no doubt, too penetrating") reverts to the sexualized imagery of the authorial penetrating imagination (*AN,* 78), thus repeating the very charge of adulterating Maisie it would refute. Sir Claude's scruple lest Maisie be tainted by "the air of . . . gross irregularity" attending the improper arrangement between her stepparents is doubled by James's praise in the preface of her capacity for "flourishing" in "the infected air," for "keeping the torch of virtue alive in an air tending infinitely to smother it" (*AN,* 149, 143).[9] Maisie's virtue is ambient, at least in James's retrospective evaluation. But the novel turns

9. Cf. the preface to *The Portrait of a Lady,* where James ascribes the moral sense of art to the quality of the "soil" and "enveloping air" of the artist's sensibility (*AN,* 45).

the same image against her, for she is said to flourish in an atmosphere "appalling to analyse."

The task of worrying over Maisie's unaccountable knowledge and uncertain moral sense is relegated to Mrs. Wix, "a dim, crooked little reflector" (*Notebooks*, 162) who parodically doubles Maisie's function as reflective center. Her "straighteners" generate a running joke about point of view; rather than correct her "divergent obliquity of vision," the straighteners clarify for others "the bearing, otherwise doubtful, of her regard" (25). The straighteners figure the novel's hoped-for "straight and sure advance to the end" (*Notebooks*, 161), the coherent narrative path that would counteract the plot's unpredictable deviations and transgressions. But Maisie's reflective consciousness creates ramifications as dubious as Mrs. Wix's oblique gaze. When she scandalizes the governess by proposing that they establish a foursome with Claude and Mrs. Beale, the impropriety charges Mrs. Wix "to the brim" like an overfull vessel of consciousness, and she replies indignantly that Maisie should "know better" (276, 271). Maisie can acquire a moral sense only by an initiation into the very knowledge that is forbidden her, and Mrs. Wix's disgusted pronouncement that Maisie is "too unspeakable" names the paradox of the novel's representational law (268, 272). For it what Maisie knows is unspeakable, and what she doesn't know "ain't worth mentioning" (101), to quote Wix herself, then her knowledge inhabits the nebulous region between the unspeakable and the unmentionable. Much like the narrator, Mrs. Wix therefore confronts the impossible task of discerning what Maisie knows without "mak[ing] her any more initiated—any 'worse' " (*Notebooks*, 162), a dilemma that doubles James's defensive concerns in the preface.

The scandal of Maisie's missing moral sense brings the narrative to a "pretty pass" (283)—the impasse brought about by the potentially fatal supersaturation of Maisie's knowledge.

> She judged that if her whole history, for Mrs. Wix, had been the successive stages of her knowledge, so the very climax of the concatenation would, in the same view, be the stage at which the knowledge should overflow. As she was condemned to know more and more, how could it logically stop before she should know Most? It came to her in fact as they sat there

on the sands that she was distinctly on the road to know Everything. She
had not had governesses for nothing; what in the world had she ever done
but learn and learn and learn? She looked at the pink sky with a placid
foreboding that she soon should have learnt All. They lingered in the
flushed air till at last it turned to grey and she seemed fairly to receive new
information from every brush of the breeze. By the time they moved
homeward it was as if this inevitability had become for Mrs. Wix a long,
tense cord, twitched by a nervous hand, on which the valued pearls of
intelligence were to be neatly strung. (281–82)

Although this passage is usually read unironically, the epiphany it announces is utterly deflated by the escalating abstractions that pretend to
mark Maisie's accession to an ever more unspeakable knowledge ("more
. . . Most . . . Everything . . . All"), capitalized as if to accentuate the
"merely" linguistic status of the narrator's claim.

Nothing more remarkable had taken place in the first heat of her own
departure, no act of perception less to be overtraced by our rough method,
than her vision . . . of the manner in which she figured. I so despair of
courting her noiseless mental footsteps here that I must crudely give you
my word for its being from this time forward a picture literally present to
her. (280–81)

The metaphor of overtracing implies that the narrator merely names an
existing preverbal cognition, but the passage goes on to posit a different
relation between language and knowledge. Maisie figures not only in the
sense denoted, but in the sense that her focalizing consciousness is constituted by the narrator's figures, figures that are not yet at her command.
The narrator's paralepsis, which elides yet posits a "picture literally present to her," interrogates the status of literal and figurative language in the
novel as a whole. For if we have access to Maisie's knowledge only
through the narrator's figures, her knowledge has no literal term, and his
relation to Maisie is one of catachresis. Despite the preface's claim to the
contrary, the figures deployed by the narrator are grounded in no prior
literal referent.

   In violation of the novel's avowed narrative strategy of a "picture restricted" to Maisie's consciousness (*AN,* 145), that consciousness is in-

voked increasingly by first-person narratorial intrusions. Since what
Maisie knew cannot, per definition, be articulated, the narrator must step
in to assure us that her knowledge outstrips even his own verbal resources.
And because each turn of events confirms the unspeakability of this
knowledge, the novel increasingly resorts to this emergency measure.
Effaced through most of the text, the narrator makes more and more
first-person interventions, but only to claim that Maisie's knowledge is
so prodigious as to resist verbalization altogether.

These narratorial interventions defy James's famous strictures against
this device in the 1883 essay on Trollope:

> He took a suicidal satisfaction in reminding the reader that the story he
> was telling was only, after all, a make-believe. He habitually referred to
> the work in hand (in the course of that work) as a novel, and to himself
> as a novelist, and was fond of letting the reader know that this novelist
> could direct the course of events according to his pleasure. . . . It is im-
> possible to imagine what a novelist takes himself to be unless he regard
> himself as an historian and his narrative as a history. It is only as an historian
> that he has the smallest *locus standi*. As a narrator of fictitious events he is
> nowhere; to insert into his attempt a backbone of logic, he must relate
> events that are assumed to be real. (*LC*, I, 1343)

In guise of the traditional gesture of presenting the novel as history, James
posits an antithesis between first-person narration and the very ground
of narrative. The "terrible *fluidity* of self-revelation," as he terms it in the
preface to *The Ambassadors* (*AN*, 321), is antithetical to the backbone or
standpoint that would ground the novel in something outside itself. The
locus standi or backbone of logic in *What Maisie Knew* is Maisie herself,
for it is Maisie's case that permits the narrative "to stand beautifully on
its feet," providing the "perfect logic" for the complications that follow
(*AN*, 142).

But the narratorial interventions of the last third of *What Maisie Knew*
participate in the suicidal element of Trollope's authorial intrusions. If
Trollope takes a suicidal satisfaction in calling attention to the artifice of
his own narrative, James involuntarily narrates the collapse of his own
locus standi, for each such intrusion shatters the illusion of the transparency

of the narrator's mediating language. The impossibility of speaking Maisie's knowledge may well threaten the narrator's existence, but it is Maisie herself who, as the novel's "ironic centre," pays for the narrator's suicidal bent by wondering to "the end, to the death—the death of her childhood," as the preface puts it (*AN,* 147, 146). This death may account for the eschatological overtones of the passage quoted above, where the culmination of Maisie's knowledge is figured as the twitching of "a long, tense cord, twitched by a nervous hand, on which the valued pearls of intelligence were to be neatly strung" (281–82). The trope of a string of pearls recurs in the critical prefaces in connection with the center of consciousness, whose lifeline or thread of consciousness is aligned with the activity of wondering that leads to death or figurative annihilation: "The range of wonderment attributed in [*In the Cage*] to the young woman employed at Cocker's differs little in essence from the speculative thread on which the pearls of Maisie's experience, in this same volume— pearls of so strange an iridescence—are mostly strung. She wonders, putting it simply, very much as Morgan Moreen wonders; and they all wonder, for that matter, very much after the fashion of our portentous little Hyacinth" (*AN,* 156). The snapping of the thread signifies the snapping or breaking of the narrative ground or basis Maisie personifies, like the "break[ing of] the chain of the girl's own consciousness" in "A London Life" (*AN,* 137).

As his notebook entries reflect, James found himself inextricably tangled in the maze of Maisie's narrative. Planned as a ten-thousand-word story,[10] *What Maisie Knew* expanded into a ninety-thousand-word novel. Yet in keeping with a characteristic Jamesian tension between the desire for complication and the demands of economy, James finds himself in an aesthetic double bind requiring infinite deferral within the constraints of form. Like Sir Claude, who begs Mrs. Wix to "be so good as to allow these horrors to terminate" (361), James is divided between his vow to "*enjamber* my period," or draw out his own narrative line, and the need for a "straight and sure advance to the end." He finds his solution in the scenic method: "the scenic scheme is the only one that *I* can trust, with

10. Fred Kaplan, *Henry James: The Imagination of Genius: A Biography* (New York, 1992), 416–17.

my tendencies, to stick to the march of an action. . . . I must now, I fully recognize, have a splendid recourse to it to see me out of the wood, at all, of this interminable little *Maisie*" (*Notebooks*, 163, 161, 167).

Despite the formalist cast of James's discussion, more is at stake here than matters of formal closure. The "march of an action" he seeks to enforce is both an underlying ground and the linear sequence of cause and effect, the "close little march of cause and effect" (*Notebooks*, 158). This (undecidable) recovery or imposition of a coherent march or sequence would yield a narrative line that could be traced to the generating source of Maisie's consciousness. Yet James can ground the narrative in Maisie's knowledge only by foregoing indirect discourse in favor of the presumptive objectivity of scene. His recourse to the scenic method promises to see him out of the wood, but also necessarily abandons the pretense that "what Maisie knew" exists prior to its articulation by the narrator. This contradiction brings the novel to a definitive representational impasse, its dialogue reduced to a series of stuttering repetitions: "She refused—she refused!" "You're free—you're free," "I know, I know!" "She hates you—she hates you," "leave her, leave her!" and so on. Like the repetitive Mrs. Wix, James's novel falls into conspicuous "iteration" (261).[11] These doubling repetitions suggestively evoke the novel's own undecidable oscillation between constative and performative theories of language, between the avowed narrative scheme outlined in the preface and the text's performative praxis. Rather than resolve the conundrum of Maisie's unspeakability, the "scenic" passages that close *What Maisie Knew* reintroduce the very conundrum they would cover over—namely, the undecidable question of whether the narrator merely represents Maisie's knowledge or brings it into being.

Nevertheless, James adduces the scenic method as "my absolute, my imperative, my *only* salvation" (*Notebooks*, 167):

Ah, this *divine* conception of one's little masses and periods in the scenic light—as rounded ACTS; this patient, pious, nobly 'vindictive' application of the scenic philosophy and method—I feel as if it still (above *all*, YET)

---

11. On James's parody in this scene of comedic convention, see Christopher Brown, "The Rhetoric of Closure in *What Maisie Knew*," *Style*, XX (1986), 58–65.

had a great deal to give me, and might carry me as far as I dream! God knows how far—into the flushed, dying day. (*Notebooks*, 162)

The light afforded by the scenic method, aligned here with James's salvific "flushed, dying day," recalls the flushed air intimating the fatal overflow of Maisie's knowledge on "the road to know Everything." This resonance points to an odd economy in which the scenic method that spells Maisie's demise as reflective center is the vehicle of James's salvation. Further, James's odd slip of "vindictive" for "vindicating" echoes the vindictive motives of Maisie's parents: "Whereas each of these persons had at first vindictively desired to keep it from the other, so at present the re-married relative sought now rather to be rid of it" (*AN*, 140). The vindictive bent of Maisie's parents is displaced onto James, or rather onto the compositional system, at once vindicating and vindictive, that both constructs' Maisie's knowledge and pushes that knowledge to its (vindictive) breaking point.

The constellation of figures in these two passages recalls a passage of "The Pupil" (1892) that proleptically images Morgan Moreen's death as a similar "flushing" into knowledge:

When he tried to figure to himself the morning twilight of childhood, so as to deal with it safely, he saw it was never fixed, never arrested, that ignorance, at the instant he touched it, was already flushing faintly into knowledge, that there was nothing that at a given moment you could say an intelligent child didn't know. It seemed to him that he himself knew too much to imagine Morgan's simplicity and too little to disembroil his tangle.[12]

Like Mrs. Wix, Pemberton is unable to straighten out the narrative tangle in which Morgan is implicated. In *The Art of the Novel*, James figures his narrative powers as "the force for which the straightener of almost any tangle is grateful while he labours" (*AN*, 146). But like the "snap of a tension" effected by Mrs. Beale's ultimatum to Sir Claude (301), this pulling at threads threatens to break the cord on which the pearls of the central intelligence are strung, fatally snapping the novel's narrative line.

12. James, *What Maisie Knew, In the Cage, The Pupil*, 547.

The flushed dying day James envisions in his notebook is a version of Morgan's flushing into knowledge—an oxymoronic "morning twilight of [his] childhood" akin to the figurative death foreseen for Maisie in the preface:

> Successfully to resist (to resist, that is, the strain of observation and the assault of experience) what would that be, on the part of so young a person, but to remain fresh, and still fresh, and to have even a freshness to communicate?—the case being with Maisie to the end that she treats her friends to the rich little spectacle of objects enbalmed in her wonder. She wonders, in other words, to the end, to the death—the death of her childhood, properly speaking; after which (with the inevitable shift, sooner or later, of her point of view) her situation will change and become another affair, subject to other measurements and with a new centre altogether. (*AN*, 146–47)

"In other words" is precisely resonant of the novel's representational scheme: it is the narrator's translation of Maisie's knowledge into other words, into figures not yet at her command, that is the agency of the death in question. The inevitable shift that produces a new center coincides not only with the death of Maisie's childhood but with the death of Maisie's point of view itself. As the narrator puts it, "She was yet to learn what it could be to recognise in some lapse of a sequence the proof of an extinction, and therefore remained unaware that this momentary pang was a foretaste of the experience of death" (291).

This compositional law is covertly expressed in the prologue, where the narrator refers to the need for a third party who could have mediated between Maisie and her parents: "What was to have been expected on the evidence was the nomination, *in loco parentis,* of some proper third person, some respectable or at least some presentable friend" (4). This expectation is realized in the unidentified lady who comes forward, in the same paragraph, to offer Maisie a home, and she delivers "a grim judgement of the whole point of view" that amounts to "an epitaph for the tomb of Maisie's childhood" (5). But this proper third person fails to mask the complicity between the novel's whole point of view and the third-person discourse of the narrator who figures Maisie's knowledge. His relation to Maisie is inherently improper, though James would have it otherwise when he indicates that Maisie's death is only and properly figurative: "She wonders, in other words . . . to the death—the death of her childhood, properly speaking" (*AN,* 146). Instead, the proper third person of the prologue calls attention to the causal connection between the death of Maisie's childhood and the novel's whole point of view, to the causal power of a narrative strategy that leaves its "infant" (*infans*) "subject strangled in that extreme of rigour" demanded by "the problem of the picture restricted" (*AN,* 145).

Something like the deathly "lapse of sequence" foreseen above comes into question with Mrs. Wix's belated attempt to impose a sequence, or coherent narrative line, on Maisie. As a figure of repression and narrative control (the narrator dryly notes that she "was not wholly directed to repression"), Wix "reduce[s] the process to sequences more definite than any it had known since the days of Moddle" (311). The passage refers to Maisie's grooming, but alludes to the need for an enforced sequence that would oppose the transgressive crossing threatening to transpire between Maisie and Sir Claude. Maisie's "vicious activity," her status as ironic center of a narrative that "works in a kind of inevitable rotary way—in what would be called a vicious circle" (*Notebooks,* 148, 74), duplicates the "same old vicious circle" (335) of adulterous crossings and realignments played out with Sir Claude and Mrs. Beale. This inevitable rotary, which parodically repeats the "rotation" of the joint custody arrangement that sets the plot in motion (*AN,* 140), threatens to bring full circle the novel's adulterous "game of going round." Mrs. Wix's command to Maisie, "Don't begin it *again!*" (297) is of no avail: thanks to her un-witting power as "centre and pretext for a fresh system of misbehaviour, a system moreover of a nature to spread and ramify" (*AN,* 143), Maisie not only reunites Mrs. Beale and Sir Claude but, Arachne-like, threatens to involve Claude in an erotic entanglement of her own.

In keeping with the novel's recurring metaphors of payment, account-ability, and settlement, the representational aporia posed by Maisie's rad-ical unspeakability is figured as an unpayable debt, an equation or math-ematical problem that defies solution. She acquires a suspicion that, had she ever in her life had a sovereign changed, would have resembled an impression, baffled by the want of arithmetic, that her change was wrong: she groped about in it that she was perhaps playing the passive part in a case of violent substitution. (301)

Here her role as token in her parents' machinations, "rebounding from racquet to racquet like a tennis ball or a shuttlecock" (*AN*, 140), converges with the economic terminology of accountability. In a reversal of the novel's initial dynamic, where Maisie is feared to be exposed to or mixed up in the compromising talk that surrounds her, she is now herself accused of "talk[ing] trash" (316). Her powers as "wonder-working agent" (*AN*, 142) are finally scandalous rather than redemptive, and she is pronounced a "monster" (189). In *The Art of the Novel*, "monstrosity" is James's term for the disjunction between originary germ and completed work that results in "comparative monsters" like *What Maisie Knew* itself (*AN*, 98). The "monstrous" tax Maisie sustains (*AN*, 150) is the price of the novel's compositional system, which produces an ironic incommensurability between the restricted economy of the reflective center and the labyrinthine amplification of the figures that translate Maisie's knowledge. Her monstrosity is the potential monstrosity of narrative, and of figurative language, itself: the novel's pervasive web and labyrinth imagery recalls Locke's figuration of rhetoric, in his discussion of "the abuse of words" in *An Essay Concerning Human Understanding*, as a "curious and inexplicable web" or "endless labyrinth." [13]

What Maisie Knew thus reaches a double impasse. Its first element is Maisie's confrontation with her unaccountable indebtedness to the narrator's figures. Its second element, which as James would say comes to the same thing, is the text's incapacity to articulate what Maisie knew in anything *but* these figures—its incapacity, that is, to name a knowledge that has no literal name. Though James's representational strategy posits a metaphorical identity between Maisie's knowledge and the narrator's figures for it, those figures put in motion a metonymical sign-sign slippage that never leads back to a literal origin or referent.

This impasse is figured by the text, precisely, *as* a figure:

13. John Locke, *An Essay Concerning Human Understanding*, ed. Alexander Campbell Fraser (1894; rpr. New York, 1959), II, 128.

The question of the settlement loomed larger to her now: it depended, she had learned, so completely on herself. Her choice, as her friend had called it, was there before her like an impossible sum on a slate, a sum that in spite of her plea for consideration she simply got off from doing while she walked about with him. (341)

This demand for a settlement of Maisie's narrative account culminates in Mrs. Wix's interrogation of her moral sense:

"*Haven't* I, after all, brought it out?" She spoke as she had never spoken even in the schoolroom and with the book in her hand.

It brought back to the child's recollection how she sometimes couldn't repeat on Friday the sentence that had been glib on Wednesday, and she dealt all feebly and ruefully with the present tough passage. Sir Claude and Mrs. Beale stood there like visitors at an "exam." She had indeed an instant a whiff of the faint flower that Mrs. Wix pretended to have plucked and now with such a peremptory hand thrust at her nose. Then it left her, and, as if she were sinking with a slip from a foothold, her arms made a short jerk. What this jerk represented was the spasm within her of something still deeper than a moral sense. She looked at her examiner; she looked at the visitors; she felt the rising of the tears she had kept down at the station. They had nothing—no, distinctly nothing—to do with her moral sense. The only thing was the old flat shameful schoolroom plea. "I don't know—I don't know."

"Then you've lost it." Mrs. Wix seemed to close the book as she fixed the straighteners on Sir Claude. "You've nipped it in the bud. You've killed it when it had begun to live." (353–54)

In keeping with the novel's mock education plot, its ethical crisis is staged as a final examination, an "inquisition of the drawing room" (56) (like the French novel scene in *The Awkward Age*) into what Maisie knows. But because her schoolroom plea of ignorance reverses her programmatic reply up to this point ("Oh I know!"), what results here is a slip from a foothold, the fall of Maisie's (and James's) *locus standi*.[14] Despite Mrs.

---

14. Cameron observes that the novel's last sentence, which attests to Wix's "wonder at what Maisie knew," "intones a form of the word 'knowledge' as it has been incanted many times earlier, but now renders its meaning definitively evasive" (*Thinking in Henry*

Beale's announcement that she and Claude "take our stand on the law" as representatives of Maisie's parents (361), the novel's representational law exposes the essential instability of the very *locus standi* it would erect. James speaks in a letter of consciousness as "something that holds one in one's place, makes it a standpoint in the universe." [15] The Jamesian center of consciousness is both the basis of such a standpoint and its vulnerability. The above "tough passage" testifies to the definitive collapse of the novel's own foothold—of its epistemological, rhetorical, and metaphysical ground or standpoint, a fall that, to invoke a Jamesian master trope, lands us in the "abyss" (360). The jerk that marks this loss of standpoint recalls Miles's fall into the abyss in *The Turn of the Screw:* "But he had already jerked straight round, stared, glared again, and seen but the quiet day. With the stroke of the loss I was so proud of he uttered the cry of a creature hurled over an abyss, and the grasp with which I recovered him might have been that of catching him in his fall." [16]

This constellation of images aligned with the Jamesian ironic center—images of loss of foothold, falling and the abyss—recalls Paul de Man's remarks on the fall as the constitutive moment of irony, marking the ironic splitting of the subject between a mystified empirical self and the self that falls into knowledge of this mystification: "The Fall, in the literal as well as the theological sense, reminds [man] of the purely instrumental, reified character of his relationship to nature. Nature can at all times treat him as if he were a thing and remind him of his factitiousness, whereas he is quite powerless to convert even the smallest particle of nature into something human." [17] The "fall" of the Jamesian ironic center, like Maisie's above, is akin to this demystification, signifying not her arrival at

---

James, 73). For a reading that complements mine in many respects, see J. Hillis Miller, *Versions of Pygmalion* (Cambridge, Mass., 1990), 23–81. This essay was composed before the appearance of Miller's work, and I have not attempted to revise it in light of the implications of his reading. My reading differs from Miller's especially in its emphasis on the indeterminacy of Maisie's knowledge as the narrator's rhetorical construction, whereas Miller emphasizes the undecidability of the ethical basis of Maisie's actions.

15.   Quoted in Georges Poulet, *The Metamorphoses of the Circle,* trans. Carley Dawson and Elliott Coleman (Baltimore, 1966), 310.

16.   Henry James, *"The Turn of the Screw" and Other Short Fiction* (Toronto, 1981), 103.

17.   De Man, *Blindness and Insight,* 214.

knowledge (despite James's title), but the text's self-reflexive marking of its procedures, which preclude an unironic presentation of the knowledge it would name.

In a parody of the novel's own settlement, Mrs. Wix appears to "close the book" on James's "slip of a girl" (*AN*, 144), enforcing a peremptory closure. She not only straightens out Maisie, but fixes her straighteners on Sir Claude. Yet her accusation lets slip the novel's narrative ruse. The usual term in James for glasses is "nippers." Strether's "eternal nippers" figure his quest for epistemological clarity in *The Ambassadors* (7); Mr. Longdon in *The Awkward Age* characteristically fixes his double eyeglass on the unprincipled frequenters of the Brookenham circle. Might there be a complicity between Mrs. Wix's straighteners and Sir Claude's alleged crime of having nipped in the bud Maisie's moral sense? To straighten Maisie out is to nip her in the bud, thanks to the equivocal moral sense of a narrative strategy that requires its heroine to wonder "to the end, to the death—the death of her childhood."

The text ultimately elides and effaces Maisie's consciousness altogether: "rigid," "dumb," and "whiter than ever" as she confronts Mrs. Wix (355), Maisie is indeed, like Hyacinth before his suicide, virtually "overpast" and "extinct." At the moment of accountability ("the moment she had had most to reckon with"), facing her surrogate parents in the circle that literalizes the vicious circle of which she is an unwitting architect, she is bereft even of the bewilderment that is her distinguishing feature as Jamesian receptive intelligence: "Bewilderment had simply gone or at any rate was going fast" (357). The novel's organizing vessel of consciousness is finally emptied out altogether.

In this articulation of Maisie's and the novel's own unaccountability, James returns us to the dilemma of the prologue. It is Beale's accountability for "a sum of which he had had the administration and of which he could render not the least account" (3) that motivates the joint custody arrangement at the novel's outset. Maisie's case thus originates in a ruptured contract that thematizes the text's obsession with its own rhetorical accountability. Like Hyacinth, who "collapses . . . overcharged with treasures of reflexion and spoils of passion of which he can give, in his poverty and obscurity, no honest account" (*AN*, 156), Maisie is "disinherited" (270), implicated in a cycle of debt and reparation in which no settlement is possible. (In a figure that explicitly recalls Hyacinth, she "was to feel henceforth as if she were flattening her nose upon the hard window-pane of the sweet-shop of knowledge," 137.) She is incommensurate, a remainder or residuum that must be sacrificed if relations are to be squared; as Sir Claude concludes, "We *can't* work her in" (360).

Maisie's fundamental indebtedness follows from her dependence on the narrator's own terms, figures in both the economic and rhetorical senses, that are not at her command. Such figures remain beyond the mastery of the Jamesian reflective center, their effects incalculable. Like Hyacinth's "lively inward revolution," the "moral revolution" ascribed to Maisie signifies a linguistic operation that is ultimately not at the command of Maisie or even of James himself. Though James would have it that the narrator merely translates Maisie's thoughts, this translation is far from innocent. As we have seen, James figures the growth of Maisie's knowledge as the progress of a letter whose delivery is perpetually deferred: thus one of her mother's curses drops into Maisie's memory "with the dry rattle of a letter falling into a pillar-box. Like the letter it was . . . delivered in due course at the right address" (14). If, like a metaphor, a translation is a transfer that creates as well as nominates, the performative effects of this translation turn out to be fatal.

It is figurative language that finally cannot be accounted for in *What Maisie Knew.* The "ironic truth" or "residuum of truth" described in the preface as "glow[ing] at the core of [James's] vision" (*AN,* 141, 142) is the residuum of language itself, of the figures which, amplifying Maisie's knowledge to an unknowable degree, remain the unknown variable in the novel's narrative equation.[18] This ironic truth is akin to the "exquisite truth" said to lurk at the "central core" of the scenic method, which entails a "roundabout and devious path" (*Notebooks,* 115) like the very vicious circle it would repair. James's "ironic centre" is thus oxymoronic

18.   Donna Przybylowicz sums up the crux of the debate about figurative language in the novel: "her . . . perceptions . . . are presented through a cross-referencing of metaphors, signifying a preverbal level of comprehension of actions and feelings that are interpreted and created by the narrator" (*Desire and Repression: The Dialectic of Self and Other in the Late Works of Henry James* [Tuscaloosa, 1986], 26). The question is precisely whether the narrator merely interprets or actually creates her perceptions; the two possibilities imply, respectively, constative and performative theories of language.

in character. In assuming an ironic distance between Maisie's knowledge and the narrator's figures for it, the reflective center can claim only an ironized centering, that is, a permanent ironic displacement of the center it posits.

According to *The Art of the Novel*, the value of the reflector is precisely its "appeal to incalculability" (*AN*, 329).[19] The Jamesian center of consciousness has incalculable, unforeseeable effects in the narratives in which it is deployed. Maisie's "death" is caused as much by the novel's representational law—what the narrator terms the "queer law of her own life" (281)—as by the psychological or intersubjective motives thematically simulated by its realistic subject. The novel's linguistic texture defies the reader's efforts to account for its overwrought, even surreal figurative language, language that cannot be attributed to Maisie and that works in a dissonant counterpoint against its neat symmetries of plot and episode.

What Maisie Knew is traditionally identified as a transitional work that looks forward to the major phase, falling in the "treacherous years" after the disappointing critical reception of *The Bostonians* and *The Princess Casamassima*.[20] James's preface contains an astonishing slip that suggests he indeed associates the novel with certain transitional anxieties: he gets its date of composition wrong by an entire decade, dating it from 1907 rather than 1897 (*AN*, 150). This retrospective falsification may reflect James's unmistakable ambivalence toward *What Maisie Knew*, but it also points to a larger gesture of appropriation in the preface itself. His discussion of *The Pupil* there digresses into a reflection on the lost "golden age" of the early American experience in Europe. James laments that these "classic years of the great Americano-European legend" remain unrepresented in American fiction:

> The comparatively brief but infinitely rich "cycle" of romance embedded
> in the earlier, the very early American reactions and returns (mediaeval in

19. Maurice Blanchot similarly writes of James's characteristic "indecipherability": "art où tout est mouvement, effort de découverte et d'investigation, plis, replis, sinuosité, réserve, art qui ne déchiffre pas, mais est le chiffre de l'indéchiffrable" (*Le Livre à venir* [Paris, 1959], 193).

20. Leon Edel designates 1895–1900 as James's "treacherous years"; see *Henry James: A Life* (New York, 1985).

the sense of being, at most, of the mid-century), what does it resemble today but a gold-mine overgrown and smothered, dislocated, and no longer workable?—all for want of the right indications for sounding, the right implements for digging, doubtless even of the right workmen, those with the right tradition and "feeling" for the job. The most extraordinary things appear to have happened, during that golden age . . . but no story of all the list was to find its just interpreter, and nothing is now more probable than that every key to interpretation has been lost. (*AN*, 153)

This remarkable passage may be considered the obverse of the famous catalogue, in *Hawthorne,* of the absent things in American life. Here it is not a rich cultural soil that is found wanting—although the mining metaphor resonates with James's complaint in 1879 about the "thin and impalpable deposit" of cultural history in America—but a writer equal to the task of representing it (*LC,* I, 352, 327). The mine is claimed to be simultaneously overworked and untouched due to the absence of "right workmen," and this contradiction points to the double movement of James's argument. For he simultaneously characterizes the golden age of Americans in Europe, the period of his own early international theme, as overworked and exhausted, thus assuming a position of belatedness in relation to his own early work, and asserts that the story of this golden age remains untold: "no story of all the list was to find its just interpreter." (The conspicuous absence in this passage is, of course, the suppressed Hawthorne himself.)

But it is precisely the gold mine of his own earlier subject matter that James was working so richly in the novels composed just prior to *The Art of the Novel.* Indeed, the implicit subject of James's metaleptic (mis)appropriation of his early career in this passage is his "reaction and return" to this transatlantic theme. By dating *Maisie* as contemporary with the critical prefaces composed between 1906 and 1908—and therefore later than *The Ambassadors, The Wings of the Dove,* and *The Golden Bowl*—James masks the return to the international theme covertly announced here. Further, his call for an interpreter of America's ongoing encounter with Europe creates imaginative space for the reinterpretation of his own "Americano-European legend" in his late great triad of novels. Along with his other major fictions of the late 1890s, *What Maisie Knew* seems to have furnished the key to James's revisionary interpretation of certain of his earlier fictions, for example the revision of *Roderick Hudson* undertaken in *The Ambassadors,* or the revisitation of *The Portrait of a Lady* that is evident in both *The Wings of the Dove* and *The Golden Bowl. What Maisie Knew* itself, for all its subdued social comedy, displays a similarly uncanny consciousness of its own narrative subterfuges that perhaps accounts for its peculiar power.

But it would be naive to look to chronology or biography to account for the novel's linguistic features. The artistic tensions adumbrated in James's preface may well find expression in *What Maisie Knew* in ways that would be difficult to define with any precision, but the relation between biography and text is not one of straightforward cause and effect. James's biography in no way furnishes a *locus standi* for later interpreters, at least in the sense of an explanatory ground or origin for his works. The concerns of *What Maisie Knew,* far from being personal, are basic to narrative, insofar as Maisie's drama as central consciousness may be read as an allegory of the duplicity of representation. "Allegory," however, is a vexed term that requires further investigation, and for this I turn to *Roderick Hudson,* James's most explicit treatment of allegory as a problematic, though perhaps also constitutive, narrative mode.

3

The Abyss of Allegory in *Roderick Hudson*

And since I am speaking critically, I may go on to say that the art of narration, in Transformation [The Marble Faun], seems to me more at fault than in the author's other novels. The story straggles and wanders, is dropped and taken up again, and towards the close lapses into an almost fatal vagueness.

—Hawthorne

At stake in James's strictures against first-person narration are, as we have seen, the *locus standi* that would authorize and stabilize the novel by grounding it in an external standpoint, origin, or telos. His 1883 Trollope essay asserts that this ground inheres in the writer's historical authority: "It is only as an historian that he has the smallest *locus standi*. As a narrator of fictitious events he is nowhere; to insert into his attempt a backbone of logic, he must relate events that are assumed to be real." James does not specify how history provides this stabilizing backbone, but it is clearly antithetical to Trollope's "suicidal" narratorial intrusions: the essay opposes first-person narration to what is called "history." It especially faults Trollope for what James terms his allegorical tendency. Allegorical tag-names, like Dr. Pessimist Anticant of *The Warden*, deprive Trollope's novels of their historical authority, effecting a "sudden disillusionment" and a shift from historicity to allegory: "we are transported from the mellow atmosphere of an assimilated Barchester to the air of ponderous allegory" (*LC*, I, 1343, 1342). Like first-person narration, allegory is seen as an imposed and arbitrary mode of signification that calls attention to its own artifice. Both are antithetical to the backbone, logic, and *locus standi* said to be provided by history.

What Maisie Knew, which at once declares and disputes the authority of its own rhetorical standpoint, suggests that the discovery or imposition of this ground is both necessary and impossible. Given that what is at stake here is the very metaphysics of narrative, what James calls allegory, as that which interferes with the text's claim to be grounded in something external to itself, appears to be something other and something more than a mode of writing that one could choose or reject at will. Such, in fact, is the burden of recent work theorizing allegory as a moment or structure constitutive of language itself.

Paul de Man provides the crucial articulation of this position. Allegory is traditionally understood as an artificial and mechanical representation of an abstract truth that could have been otherwise expressed. In the Romantic critique of allegory exemplified by Coleridge, allegory is a system of signification in which the relation between signifier and signified is wholly arbitrary or conventional, as against symbol, which claims an organic connection or other natural resemblance between the two. De Man understands this problem of noncoincidence between idea and representation as characteristic of the structure of the linguistic sign itself, which displays a similar discontinuity between sign and meaning. Because allegory calls attention to the temporal discontinuity between the transcendental idea and its representation, it challenges both the symbol's illusion of simultaneity and "the very possibility of a text governed by a preconceived, self-contained idea."[1]

James's own critical language is heavily colored by the Romantic understanding of allegory as an arbitrary and mechanical mode of signification. In *Hawthorne,* allegory is aligned with the diminishing "thinness" and "blankness" of Hawthorne's style. Both there and in the Trollope

---

1. This formulation is Ewa Ziarek's; see her lucid summary of the critical reevaluation of allegory in " 'Surface Stratified on Surface': A Reading of Ahab's Allegory," *Criticism,* XXXI (1989), 271–86. The key de Man texts are *Blindness and Insight* and *Allegories of Reading;* see also J. Hillis Miller, *Hawthorne and History* (Cambridge, Mass., 1991). On Jamesian allegory, see Esch, " 'Understanding Allegories': Reading *The Portrait of a Lady.*"

essay, allegory is negatively valorized, yet invoked at pivotal argumentative moments. James's most explicit treatment of allegory may well be *Roderick Hudson,* an early novel that conspicuously meditates on Hawthorne. Its eponymous hero stands in for Hawthorne himself, as I shall argue, and Roderick's artistic failure stages a simultaneous rejection and incorporation of Hawthornian allegory. I wish here to explore one region of *Roderick Hudson*'s affiliation with *The Marble Faun,* its most prominent Hawthornian intertext:[2] the problematic and fallen status of allegory itself.

Roderick Hudson reopens the questions of aesthetic transmission thematized in *The Marble Faun,* which is haunted by a sense of the belatedness of an indigenous American art. Miriam argues that sculpture is an exhausted art form and sculptors "the greatest plagiarists in the world": "sculpture has no longer a right to claim any place among living arts. It has wrought itself out, and come fairly to an end."[3] Rome figures the paralyzing presence of history, whose burden is embodied in Hilda, the painter who, after her arrival in Rome, is reduced to copying masterpieces in the Pinacoteca. And though the novel speculates that originality remains possible in America, where each generation reinvents itself (220), Hawthorne's preface famously laments the impossibility of writing romance in America, "a country where there is no shadow, no antiquity, no mystery, no picturesque and gloomy wrong, nor anything but a commonplace prosperity" (vi).

A similar anxiety of originality colors *Hawthorne,* which both quotes and echoes this passage in James's notorious enumeration of "the items of high civilization, as it exists in other countries, which are absent from the texture of American life"—the "negative side" of the indigenous culture that had been available to Hawthorne:

2. See Sanford E. Marovitz, "*Roderick Hudson:* James's *Marble Faun,*" *Texas Studies in Literature and Language,* XI (1970), 1427–43, and Richard Brodhead, *The School of Hawthorne* (New York, 1986), perhaps the finest and fullest study of James's continuing revisitation of Hawthorne. On James's place in the American tradition of belatedness vis-à-vis Britain in particular, see Robert Weisbuch, *Atlantic Double-Cross: American Literature and British Influence in the Age of Emerson* (Chicago, 1986), 275–95.

3. Nathaniel Hawthorne, *The Marble Faun* (1860; New York, 1961), 95.

No State, in the European sense of the word, and indeed barely a specific national name. No sovereign, no court, no personal loyalty, no aristocracy, no church, no clergy, no army, no diplomatic service, no country gentlemen, no palaces, no castles, nor manors, nor old country-houses, nor parsonages, nor thatched cottages nor ivied ruins; no cathedrals, nor abbeys, nor little Norman churches; no great Universities nor public schools—no Oxford, nor Eton, nor Harrow; no literature, no novels, no museums, no pictures, no political society, no sporting class—no Epsom nor Ascot! (*LC,* I, 351–52)

In its extended homage to Hawthorne's own complaint, this passage conspicuously misreads James's indebtedness to Hawthorne as an intrinsic American cultural poverty.[4] *Hawthorne* internalizes *The Marble Faun*'s myth of the fall: the Civil War, by which America has "eaten of the tree of knowledge," marks the fortunate fall that makes possible James's own advent, and Hawthorne is figured in an essay of 1872 as a prelapsarian innocent, "the last pure American" who exemplifies "a simpler and less encumbered civilization." Hawthorne thus figures the double bind of nineteenth-century American art: disabled by the cultural poverty asserted in *Hawthorne,* he is yet said to have "forfeited a precious advantage in ceasing to tread his native soil," incurring "that penalty of seeming factitious and unauthoritative, which is always the result of an artist's attempt to project himself into an atmosphere in which he has not a transmitted and inherited property" (*LC,* I, 428, 313–14, 444, 445). Like Roderick, James's Hawthorne is unable to realize his artistic potential either inside or outside of America. In the legacy projected by this narrative, Hawthorne's (and Roderick's) deracinated relation to Europe is transumed by James, who plays Christ to Hawthorne's Adam in this implicit typological scheme.

The same dynamic unfolds in James's reading of *The Marble Faun* as

4. Ian F. A. Bell points out that James's citation of Hawthorne's preface, by quoting the single sentence, decontextualizes and simplifies the argument of the passage: "Hawthorne's position in this Preface is by no means straightforward, and it is part of the function of James's erasure to render it more reductive than it is for the sake of his wider argument which will restore its complications in James's own terms" (*Henry James and the Past: Readings into Time* [Houndmills, U.K., 1991], 40).

played out in *Roderick Hudson*. For James, as for Hawthorne, Rome is "weighted with a crushing past" imaged as diseased and pestilential, "an atmosphere so heavily weighted with echoes and memories one grows to believe that there is nothing in one's consciousness that is not fore-doomed to moulder and crumble and become dust for the feet, and possible malaria for the lungs, of future generations."[5] Saturated as it is with echoes both of *The Marble Faun* (to say nothing of *Middlemarch*) and of Turgenev's *On the Eve* (1860), another novel preoccupied with a thematics of belatedness, such a passage exemplifies the dilemma it diagnoses. *Roderick Hudson* turns on the question of whether Roderick will develop artistic autonomy or be reduced to the stature of mere copyist, like Hilda. His first statue, the copy of the Greek water-drinker, indeed actualizes the "plagiarism" Miriam belittles. Gloriani predicts that the Greek bronze represents a dead end; he tells Roderick, "It's deucedly pretty. . . . But, my dear young friend, you can't keep this up." Roderick's artistic nationalism appears a transparent reaction-formation to the prevailing sense of belatedness: "We stand like a race with shrunken muscles, staring helplessly at the weights our forefathers easily lifted" (244, 243).

Central to the novel's troubled articulation of James's own anxiety of belatedness is its use of Rowland Mallet as center of consciousness. The preface notes, "The centre of interest throughout 'Roderick' is in Rowland Mallet's consciousness, and the drama is the very drama of that consciousness." In keeping with the double requirement of the reflective center, Rowland is "acute," yet also "bedimmed and befooled and bewildered." As the reflector whose "view and experience" of Roderick shapes the narrative, Rowland is both witness and author of his protégé's literal and figurative "collapse" (*AN,* 16, 15).

Mallet's surname both points to this instrumentality and links him to Striker and Spooner of Roderick's disdained Northhampton law firm, whose names comedically project Rowland's ambivalent, contradictory stick-and-carrot approach toward his charge. (It is no accident that Rod-

5. *Roderick Hudson,* in *Novels 1871–1880* (New York, 1983), 344, 278. All quotations of the 1875 edition are from this text; all quotations of the 1908 New York Edition are from *Roderick Hudson* (Oxford, 1980), hereinafter referred to parenthetically as NY.

erick uses a mallet to destroy the bust of Striker in announcing his rejection of the law in favor of sculpture.) Mallet further puns on the diminutive of "malle" or trunk, when before their departure for Rome, Roderick taps his forehead and cries, "What I am to take with me I carry here," while Rowland thinks ruefully of "the light stowage, in his own organism, of the region indicated by Roderick, and of the heavy one in deposit at his banker's, of bags and boxes" (197). The joke about physical and intellectual baggage both activates Mallet's punning surname and underlines the vicariousness and mimetic desire that govern their relation.[6] Rowland identifies in Roderick a surrogate who will lend "a reflected usefulness" to his life: he declares, "if I'm not a producer, I shall at any rate be an observer" (199, 216). Rowland's delicate scruples toward Cecilia, which make "charity difficult and patronage impossible," prove inoperative with Roderick. Roderick's own gift for "appropriat[ing] what came to his hand," which complements his patron's willing instrumentality, facilitates this equivocal symbiosis (167, 182).

Rowland's protestation that "I don't understand double people" (435) therefore belies the premise of this symbiotic vicarious doubling, underlined too by Roderick's grievance about having been consigned to "fill a double place" (194) since his brother's death. Further, Rowland's "moral passion" for Roderick (308) is overdetermined by its doubly aesthetic and erotic character—an overdetermination revealed when he describes the "inspiration" he longs for, explaining that "I am waiting till something takes my fancy irresistibly," and Cecilia deduces, "What an immense number of words . . . to say you want to fall in love!" (169, 171). She responds to this profession by introducing Roderick in the form of his bronze, which she presents with the preface, "if I refused last night to show you a pretty girl, I can at least show you a pretty boy"

6. René Girard, *Deceit, Desire, and the Novel: Self and Other in Literary Structure*, trans. Yvonne Freccero (Baltimore, 1965). The mimetic quality of Roderick and Christina's relations is also noted by Armstrong (*The Phenomenology of Henry James*, 83–84), and by Cameron, who describes the "fusion" of consciousness produced by the fragmentation, incompletion, and insufficient differentiation of character in the novel (*Thinking in Henry James*, 45–50). For Cameron, James's identification of Mallet as central consciousness is a retrospective attempt to compensate for this diffusion of character.

(177). Rowland's genius is "altogether imitative" (169) in more ways than one: in keeping with the conventions of Girardian mediated desire,[7] Rowland and Roderick are even in love with the same woman—Mary Garland, to whom Roderick proposes on the eve of their departure. The proposal is itself inadvertently precipitated by Rowland, to whom Roderick explains, "you came and put me into such ridiculous good-humor that I felt an extraordinary desire to tell some woman that I adored her" (220).[8]

The logic of this erotic mediation is established in the novel's opening paragraph, where the narrator explains Rowland's failure to marry his cousin's widow Cecilia:

> It was not that the young man disliked her; on the contrary, he regarded her with a tender admiration, and he had not forgotten how, when his cousin had brought her home on her marriage, he had seemed to feel the upward sweep of the empty bough from which the golden fruit had been plucked, and had then and there accepted the prospect of bachelorhood. (167)

Rowland synecdochically renounces women in general on the basis of this metaleptic "loss" of Cecilia, and the novel replays this renunciation in the Mary Garland subplot, whose triangulated relations are governed by Rowland's desire to "be" Roderick. His "vicarious resentment" of Roderick's infidelity to Mary is itself oriented toward his homosocial/ homoerotic bond with Roderick, whom he convinces to maintain the engagement as "a kind of personal favor" (NY, 159, 477).

Although encouraged by Roderick's obsession with Christina to ponder his own chances with her, Rowland concludes that "Mary Garland was not a person to put up, at any point, with what might be called the princess's leavings" (460). In 1908, this passage was elaborated to read:

---

7. Eve Kosofsky Sedgwick, *Between Men: English Literature and Male Homosocial Desire* (New York, 1985), especially 1–27.

8. His inadvertent mediation has a precedent in Turgenev's *On the Eve,* in which Bersenyev unwittingly brings together Elena, the woman he loves, and Insarov; as Bersenyev says, "it seems as though it had been decreed at my birth that I should be a go-between." See *On the Eve,* trans. Constance Garnett (London, 1973), 77.

Was the old understanding "off," or was Mary, in spite of humiliation, keeping it on?—was she in short consenting to *that,* to humiliation? Rowland looked at the question rather than asked it, since everything hung for him on her possible appetite for sacrifice, on his measure, so to call it, of what she would abjectly 'take.' Was she one of those who would *be* abject for some last scrap of the feast of their dream? It wronged her, as he liked to think of her, to believe either that she was or that she wasn't. (NY, 331)

Rowland's double-binding, damned-if-she-does-and-damned-if-she-doesn't logic here is characteristic. If Mary remains abject in the face of Roderick's infidelity, her appetite for sacrifice requires her rejection of Rowland. But if she throws over Roderick in favor of Rowland, she would fail to behave like Rowland himself, therefore violating the implicit code according to which all desire in the novel is routed through Roderick. Rowland's "unreliability" as central intelligence is underlined by James's pointed ironization of his third-person perspective in the New York edition, where his fantasy that Mary had "'transferred her esteem' to him" (NY, 350) is exposed as a narcissistic transference of his own.[9] But it is Rowland himself who proves unwilling to put up with another's leavings: just as his fancy for Cecilia dies a "natural death" along with his cousin, so his "reversionary interest" in Mary is obstructed by Roderick's posthumous mediation in the form of her "loud, tremendous cry" at the sight of Roderick's body, a cry that relegates Rowland to the status of Roderick's leavings (167, 371, 511). Roderick even interposes posthumously between Rowland and the always already disqualified Cecilia: when Rowland visits her in Northhampton, "he talks to her of Roderick, of whose history she never wearies and whom he never elsewhere names" (NY, 389).

In its documentation of Roderick's decline, the novel posits three distinct theories of "genius" or artistic production: as a finite commodity susceptible to misuse or overexpenditure; as a mysterious agency of in-

---

9. As Sacvan Bercovitch observes, James's revisions for the New York Edition almost invariably ironize Rowland's perspective or emphasize his self-interest ("The Revision of Rowland Mallet," *Nineteenth-Century Fiction,* XXIV [1969], 210–21). See also Philip Horne's chapter on *Roderick Hudson* in *Henry James and Revision: The New York Edition* (Oxford, 1990), the fullest account as yet of the New York Edition and James's revision practices.

spiration exterior to the self; and as a mechanism, understood alternately as an instrument of the will or, in more naturalistic terms, as a machine-like function beyond individual control. The first theory is invoked by Rowland's account of his charge's failure of inspiration, also an ironic reminiscence of the bronze water-drinker: "The bottle won't pour; he turns it upside down; it's no use! Sometimes he declares it's empty—that he has done all he was made to do" (359). The narrator similarly speculates that an "essential spring had dried up within him" (456). This view of genius as an expendable life force also resonates with the theory of Roderick's talent as a watch or other mechanism. Rowland reflects that "we must live as our pulses are timed, and Roderick's struck the hour very often," yet fears that Roderick is "living too fast" (225). The metaphor is finally picked up by Roderick himself: "What if the watch should run down," he asked, "and you should lose the key? What if you should wake up some morning and find it stopped, inexorably, appallingly stopped?" (315). Rowland indeed observes Roderick's final decline by waiting "grimly and doggedly, suppressing an imprecation as, from time to time, one looked at one's watch" (456). The reliable Singleton, by contrast, is "a watch that never runs down" (483). Roderick's figure of the key as antidote to the mechanical failure of genius proves proleptic. Rowland early declares himself a "man of genius, half-finished" who spends his days "groping for the latch of a closed door," and he repeats the figure in his diagnosis of Roderick's character flaw: "I suppose there is some key or other to his character, but I try in vain to find it; and yet I can't believe that Providence is so cruel as to have turned the lock and thrown the key away" (171, 358). But throwing the key away is exactly what Rowland himself does: immediately after the confrontation that precipitates Roderick's fatal fall, he discovers that his keys are missing (503). As Roderick's "specially patented agent of Providence" (252), Rowland is himself the architect of Roderick's ultimate mechanical failure. He rationalizes, "I have done my best, and if the machine is running down I have a right to stand aside and let it scuttle" (358). There may be a connection here to the figure of the key in *Hawthorne,* where James praises Hawthorne for his "ease . . . in the moral, psychological realm; he goes to and fro in it, as a man who knows his way. His tread is a light and modest one, but he keeps the key in his pocket" (*LC,* I, 368). Hawthorne's "key" to "the deeper psychology" is opposed to his penchant for mechanical allegory. As we have seen, the figure of the key in the preface to *What Maisie Knew* implicitly stands in for Hawthorne: James's speculation that "every key to interpretation has been lost" in the representation of nineteenth-century America strategically glosses over Hawthorne's contribution to the "classic years of the great Americano-European legend" (*AN*, 153).

The several theories of genius invoked by Rowland to explain Roderick's decline ultimately acquire a kind of causal power to produce it, for in his interpretive capacity as reflective center, Rowland is instrumental in Roderick's fall. His reservations about the course of self-improvement planned for his own sojourn in Rome prove proleptic:

> "It's all very well, but I have a distinct prevision of this—that if Roman life doesn't do something substantial to make you happier, it increases tenfold your liability to moral misery. It seems to me a rash thing for a sensitive soul deliberately to cultivate its sensibilities by rambling too often among the ruins of the Palatine, or riding too often in the shadow of the aqueducts." (171)

But this program of self-cultivation is precisely what he prescribes for Roderick. Further, his patronage is predicated upon Roderick's vulnerability to the burden of the artistic past figured by Rome. He responds as follows to Roderick's first failure of inspiration:

> He was in the situation of a man who has been riding a blood horse at an even, elastic gallop, and of a sudden feels him stumble and balk. As yet, he reflected, he had seen nothing but the sunshine of genius; he had forgotten that it has its storms. Of course it had! And he felt a flood of comradeship rise in his heart which would float them both safely through the worst weather. (249)

In the New York Edition, this passage becomes:

> He was in the situation of a man who had been riding a blood-horse at a steady elastic gallop and of a sudden felt him stumble or shy. But he bethought himself that if half the "lift" of intercourse with Roderick was

his having fine nerves he himself had no right to enjoy the play of the machine—which was quite definitely what he did enjoy—without some corresponding care for it and worry about it. He immediately recognised the present hour as the very ground of his original act. (NY, 93)

Roderick's stumble ratifies Rowland's interest and provides the metaleptic "ground" of his patronage. The "play of the machine" invokes the mechanism of Roderick's genius as figured by the watch metaphor—the mechanism whose deficiency is assumed from the start. Roderick is "fallen" and a "dead failure" well before his fall makes it official: he speaks of his "dead" affection for Mary, his "dead ambitions," his "poor dead brain" (451; NY, 314, 400, 460, 465).

Like the "fatal fall" of Miriam's persecutor in *The Marble Faun* (127), Roderick's fall from the cliff appears the outcome of wish-fulfillment: much as the glance exchanged between Miriam and Donatello sanctions Donatello's murderous impulse, so Roderick's fall literalizes Rowland's figurative constructions. He warns Roderick, "You are standing on the edge of a gulf. If you suffer anything that has passed to interrupt your work on that figure, you take your plunge" (365). Roderick's declaration to his mother and Mary of his artistic failure is accordingly imaged as a "fatal plunge" (444)—the plunge literalized by his "inevitable slip" and "fall[ ] from a great height" (510, 509). The fall is explicitly prefigured by Rowland's constructions as central intelligence:

His idea persisted; it clung to him like a sturdy beggar. The sense of the matter, roughly expressed, was this: If Roderick was really going, as he himself had phrased it, to "fizzle out," one might help him on the way— one might smooth the *descensus Averno*. For forty-eight hours there swam before Rowland's eyes a vision of Roderick, graceful and beautiful as he passed, plunging, like a diver, from an eminence into a misty gulf. The gulf was destruction, annihilation, death; but if death was decreed, why should not the agony be brief? (371)

This passage, whose introductory simile pointedly recalls Miriam's clinging persecutor, aestheticizes Rowland's fantasy by assimilating it to a Virgilian descent to the underworld. Like his later premonitions of the storm and of a "fatal plunge" having been taken, the passage proleptically and coercively figures Roderick's fall (444). Roderick fatally repeats the Baden episode, which Rowland images as "one of the plunges, really touching bottom, that the plunger with the brine of the deep sea in his mouth doesn't need, or never has wind again, to repeat" (NY, 104).

Rowland's status as reflective center thus affords him considerable narrative power as "agent of Providence" (252). Roderick's complaint to his patron, "I resent the range of your vision pretending to be the limit of my action," precisely designates the relation between narrative strategy and causality in the novel (496). As the self-designated "hidden Providence" who "comes upon the scene at critical moments," Rowland is a kind of narrator who causally intervenes in the events he recounts. The "tension of the watcher and the time-keeper" he detects in Mary is indeed a projection of his own role as spectator to the "sad spectacle" of Roderick's demise (NY, 332; 457). But if Roderick's fall is readable as the exorcism by his beleaguered double, the text posits an alternative interpretation.

Both Rowland and James's narrator interpret Roderick's case as a study of failed will. The narrator emphasizes his forehead's "want of breadth," a physiognomy that implies a fatal character disorder and objectifies the flawed "mechanism" of his genius (181); Roderick indeed develops the mannerism of dramatically pressing his hand to his forehead. (In a conflation of this gesture and the watch metaphor, he declares his "conviction that if the hour strikes *here*," and he tapped his forehead, "I shall disappear, dissolve, be carried off in a cloud!" [316]—an ironic "assumption" and the inverse of his actual fate.) Rowland concludes that "it was essentially vain to appeal to the poor fellow's will; there was no will left; its place was an impotent void." Even Roderick encourages the theory that he is driven by "a restless fiend" or "restless demon within," that he is "incomplete" and "helpless in the grasp of his temperament" (474, 180, 334, 310). He offers the hypothesis that "there is a certain group of circumstances possible for every man, in which his will is destined to snap like a dry twig," and Rowland accordingly frets that his protégé may be "brittle" (258, 317). Both Rowland and Roderick intermittently endorse the narrator's line of interpretation by reading Roderick's downfall as an allegorical narrative of the will:[10] his fall into the abyss indeed

10.   On Rowland's allegorical propensity, see Peter J. Conn, "*Roderick Hudson:* The

literalizes his figure for the will as "an abyss of abysses" (NY, 103). Most conspicuous is Rowland's own allegorical propensity, as in his reading of the "picturesque symbolism" of the artists gathered at Gloriani's soirée: Roderick represents "a genius which combined sincerity with power," Gloriani "art with a worldly motive, skill unleavened by faith," Singleton "an embodiment of aspiring candor" (247).

The novel posits Christina Light as the catalyst who activates Roderick's latent character flaw. Madame Grandoni's cautionary tale about the painter ruined by his passion for a Roman model provides the obvious setup for this reading; Christina's introduction neatly coincides with Roderick's resumption of work after his riotous summer at Baden-Baden, thus furnishing the fatal obstacle to Roderick's success. When Roderick is back in his studio, it is not inspiration that comes knocking ("This name, however, for a possible knock at his door, what was it, truly, but another word for an inspiration?" [NY, 348]). At the sound of the bell, Roderick cries, "Talk of the devil . . . and you see his horns!" (263): his proverb invokes Christina as a quasi-allegorical figure, and so identifies her as the narrative device that deflects the plot from Roderick's aesthetic blockage to a dilemma of the will. Her seductiveness is figured in images of engulfment (287–88), thus aligning her with Roderick's fatal plunge.

The allegorical cast assigned Roderick's story is curious in view of James's strictures against allegory in the Trollope essay and especially in *Hawthorne.* There, James denigrates Hawthorne's allegorical bent as a symptom of his naive and provincial "charm":

> Hawthorne, in his metaphysical moods, is nothing if not allegorical, and allegory, to my sense, is quite one of the lighter exercises of the imagination. . . . The only cases in which it is endurable is when it is extremely spontaneous, when the analogy presents itself with eager promptitude.

Role of the Observer," *Nineteenth-Century Fiction,* XXVI (1971), 65–82. Many readings of the novel have been colored by the text's allegorical self-interpretation; the most illuminating of these include Armstrong, *The Phenomenology of Henry James;* Kenneth Graham, *Henry James: The Drama of Fulfillment* (Oxford, 1975), 29–57; and Linda Lohn, " 'An Abyss of Abysses': Will, Morality, and Artistic Imagination in James's *Roderick Hudson,*" *Henry James Review,* XII (1991), 93–100.

When it shows signs of having been groped and fumbled for, the needful illusion is of course absent and the failure complete. Then the machinery alone is visible, and the end to which it operates becomes a matter of indifference. (*LC,* I, 366–67)

Like Trollope's first-person intrusions, allegory is damaging for its self-reflexive exposure of the text's own machinery. The passage invokes the Coleridgean categories of allegory and symbol, in which symbol is the privileged term, allegory the fallen, secondary, and derivative term.[11] For James, as for Coleridge, allegory is an arbitrary and mechanical narrative mode; in the *Biographia Literaria* Coleridge consistently speaks of it in mechanical metaphors, as opposed to the organic metaphors that convey symbol's organic and synecdochic participation in its referent.[12] Coleridge, we recall, aligns symbol with the imagination, and allegory with the inferior faculty of fancy. James accordingly views Hawthorne as "a man of fancy"—indeed, Hawthorne is said to exemplify the distinction between fancy and the imagination (*LC,* I, 365, 373), and "fancy" is a key term in *Roderick Hudson,* applied both to Roderick's waning inspiration and to his infatuation with Christina.

Roderick's decline is pointedly linked to the increasingly allegorical character of his work. He projects a series of sculptures based on abstract themes (Beauty, Power, Wisdom, Genius) in what Gloriani calls "the transcendental style," predicated upon a theory of "divine forms" that aspires to represent "beauty of Type" (261, 243; NY, 86).[13] Against Roderick's understanding of art as the formal embodiment of the idea, the novel identifies Gloriani's theory of representation as pure formal manipulation based on an assumed disjunction between image and idea: "It was the artist's opinion . . . that it is a waste of wit to nurse metaphysical

---

11.   On the Romantic valorization of symbol over allegory and their correlative organic and mechanical metaphors, see de Man, "The Rhetoric of Temporality," in *Blindness and Insight,* 187–228.

12.   Samuel Taylor Coleridge, *Selected Poetry and Prose of Coleridge,* ed. Donald A. Stauffer (New York, 1951), 109–428, especially 257–69.

13.   His idealism perhaps associates him with the idealistic-allegorical style of such Hudson River School artists as Thomas Cole and Asher Durand; see Barbara Novak, *American Painting of the Nineteenth Century: Realism, Idealism, and the American Experience* (New York, 1979).

distinctions, and a sadly meagre entertainment to caress imaginary lines; that the thing to aim at is the expressive, and the way to reach it is by ingenuity; that for this purpose everything may serve" (237). Roderick's naive transcendental style proves his undoing; as he complains, "I haven't an idea. I think of subjects, but they remain mere lifeless names. They are mere words—they are not images" (263). Recalling Coleridge's denigration of allegory in *The Stateman's Manual* as "but a translation of abstract notions into a picture language," [14] Roderick gets stuck in a mode of allegorical abstraction that yields only lifeless names lacking material embodiment. He encounters the impasse of allegory itself: the fatal disjunction between image and word that calls attention to the arbitrary and mechanical relation between allegorical vehicle and tenor. Leavenworth's commission of the allegorical representation of Culture parodies this dilemma, for it is this project that brings Roderick definitively "face to face with the dead blank of my mind" (313). In a realization of his complaint that artists are expected to be "mere machines," Roderick even acquires a "mechanical" meekness that aligns him with the mechanical character of allegory (311; NY, 347). His sculpture duplicates the "blankness," "the stiff and mechanical" properties imputed to allegory in *Hawthorne* (*LC,* I, 351, 368). The "blank and stony face" of the cliff that rises above Roderick's corpse (510) reproduces both this blankness and the inexpressive stoniness of the "stone dead" model in *The Marble Faun* (130). Indeed, Singleton's homage inadvertently divines Roderick's ultimate reification into an impassive emblem of his own lifeless art: "In my memories of this Roman artist-life, he will be the central figure. He will stand there in radiant relief, as beautiful and unspotted as one of his own statues!" (439).

The text's ambivalent invocation of Hawthorne may be the burden, too, of the two flower vignettes—the scene at the Colosseum between Roderick and Christina, and its repetition with Rowland and Mary. In each case, the attempt to pick the elusive flower represents the danger of an "ugly fall" (472). We are reminded of the famous passage from *Hawthorne:*

14. Quoted by Angus Fletcher, *Allegory: The Theory of a Symbolic Mode* (1964; rpr. Ithaca, 1982), 16n29.

But our author must accept the awkward as well as the graceful side of his fame; for he has the advantage of pointing a valuable moral. This moral is that the flower of art blooms only where the soil is deep, that it takes a great deal of history to produce a little literature, that it needs a complex social machinery to set a writer in motion. American civilization has hitherto had other things to do than to produce flowers. . . . Three or four beautiful talents of trans-Atlantic growth are the sum of what the world usually recognises, and in this modest nosegay the genius of Hawthorne is admitted to have the rarest and sweetest fragrance. (*LC*, I, 320)

In "The Madonna of the Future" (1875), the relative thinness of American culture is similarly figured as barren soil, and American expatriation signifies a "perpetual exile" from "the prime of art." [15] The crux of *Roderick Hudson* is the problem of producing the flower of art in defiance of this aesthetic belatedness. Cecilia predicts that Roderick will "put forth some wonderful flowers," and Rowland relishes his "serene efflorescence" (NY, 38, 228). But the trope of the flower is linked to a fatal fall—the very "principle of collapse" Roderick is said to exemplify in the preface (*AN*, 13). Ironically, James's trope enacts the intertextual anxiety it would master, for as Pamela Schirmeister observes, Hawthorne's preface to *Mosses from an Old Manse* repeatedly tropes his own tales as flowers. [16]

Roderick thus becomes a figure for Hawthorne himself, the doomed precursor who plays out the via negativa of James's own controlled, mediated, and transumptive relation to tradition (as projected in *Hawthorne*). Rowland's complicity in his protégé's fall identifies him to this extent with James, an identification noted in T. S. Eliot's complaint that in *Roderick Hudson* James "commits the cardinal sin of failing to 'detect' one

15.   Henry James, *The Reverberator, Madame de Mauves, A Passionate Pilgrim, and Other Tales* (1908; rpr. New York, 1936), 442, 440, Vol. XIII of *The Novels and Tales of Henry James*. Like *Roderick Hudson*, "The Madonna of the Future" offers a parable of James's own anxiety of influence in relation to both Hawthorne and his English and Continental forebears: the narrator's unnamed interlocutor, who articulates the story's theory of American belatedness, is designated as H——.

16.   Pamela Schirmeister, *The Consolations of Space: The Place of Romance in Hawthorne, Melville, and James* (Stanford, 1990), 143.

of his own characters." [17] We can now begin to understand the causality of what the narrator terms Roderick's "inevitable slip" (510). This inevitability goes a long way toward explaining the novel's odd causal dynamics, whose law appears to be that Roderick falls because everyone predicts he will: as the narrator remarks, "When one is looking for symptoms one easily finds them" (491). Roderick's death fixes and arrests his allegorical meaning; he "must" fall in order to vindicate the allegorical reading posited by both Rowland and the narrator. Rowland's exclamation to Mary Garland, "*Quod erat demonstrandum!*" (473) could be the motto of this logic of causality: the given of Roderick's flawed mechanism yields the structure of a Q.E.D.

The questions of originality and belatedness that *Roderick Hudson* inherits from *The Marble Faun* are dropped, at least thematically. The novel swerves in midcourse from an inquiry into the burden of the American artist in the nineteenth century to an allegory of the will. But James's exorcism of Hawthorne takes the form of allegory itself. Rowland's fantasy of Roderick's plunge into a gulf of death and destruction, for instance, is read by Rowland himself as an allegorical repetition of the temptation of Christ (373). Further, the confrontation that provokes Roderick's ambiguously suicidal accident turns on Rowland's pronouncement that his protégé is "a perfect egotist." He reflects that "Reality was never so consistent as that!": Roderick's "supreme . . . expression" of "the insolence of egotism" is allegorical in its consistency (499, 498). This vignette makes explicit the novel's reminiscence of Hawthorne's 1843 story "Egotism; or, the Bosom Serpent," about a sculptor named Roderick Elliston who is consumed from within by an allegorical serpent. [18] The novel recalls this Hawthornian intertext in Mrs. Light's lamentation of Christina's ingratitude: "To have nourished a serpent, sir, all these years! to have lavished one's self upon a viper that turns and stings her own poor mother!" (426). Significantly, James singles out "The Bosom Serpent" in *Hawthorne* as exemplifying the infelicity of Hawthorne's more allegorical fictions: "Certainly, as a general thing, we are

17. T. S. Eliot, "On Henry James," in *The Question of Henry James,* ed. F. W. Dupee (New York, 1945), 108–19, 117.

18. Nathaniel Hawthorne, *Mosses from an Old Manse* (Columbus, Ohio, 1974), 268–83, Vol. X of *The Centenary Edition of the Works of Nathaniel Hawthorne.*

struck with the ingenuity and felicity of Hawthorne's analogies and cor-
respondences; the idea appears to have made itself at home in them easily.
. . . But in such things as *The Birth-Mark* and *The Bosom-Serpent,* we are
struck with something stiff and mechanical, slightly incongruous, as if
the kernel had not assimilated its envelope" (*LC,* I, 367–68).

The novel's allegorical cast, and its indebtedness to "The Bosom Serpent" in particular, may be what is at stake in James's identification of
the alleged structural flaw of *Roderick Hudson,* the novel's time scheme:
Roderick's decline, he worries, is too abrupt to be plausible.[19]

> It stared me in the face that the time-scheme of the story is quite inade-
> quate, and positively to that degree that the fault but just fails to wreck it.
> The thing escapes, I conceive, with its life: the effect sought is fortunately
> more achieved than missed, since the interest of the subject bears down,
> auspiciously dissimulates, this particular flaw in the treatment. . . . My
> mistake on Roderick's behalf—and not in the least of conception, but of
> composition and expression—is that, at the rate at which he falls to pieces,
> he seems to place himself beyond our understanding and our sympathy.
> (*AN,* 12)

The novel may escape with its life, but this is more than one can say for
Roderick himself who, as James's mischievous literalism registers, literally
as well as figuratively falls to pieces. However, James misprises the mistake
in question; the developmental foreshortening diagnosed here is the effect not of the novel's time scheme, as the passage claims, but of the
novel's confusion of realism and allegory, of the "principle of development" and the "principle of collapse" (*AN,* 13) contrasted in the preface—the latter principle actualized by Roderick's fall. The requirements
of verisimilitude James invokes are irrelevant, for Roderick's fall is not
realistic, but allegorical. Yet while the novel manages to elude the formal
equivalent of Roderick's fall, its foreshortened time scheme remains, for
James, a potential abyss.

19.   As often in the reception of the novels, critics have been too quick to take James
at his word, and *Roderick Hudson* (along with the almost entirely neglected early novels,
Watch and Ward and *Confidence*) has not received the attention it deserves. Oscar Cargill
correctly observes that James's own denigration of the novel "has been detrimental to its
prestige and to its evaluation" (*The Novels of Henry James* [New York, 1961], 24).

This eternal time-question is accordingly, for the novelist, always there and always formidable; always insisting on the *effect* of the great lapse and passage, of the "dark backward and abysm". . . . What I clung to as my principle of simplification was the precious truth that I was dealing, after all, essentially with an Action, and that no action, further, was ever made historically vivid without a certain factitious compactness; though this logic indeed opened up horizons and abysses of its own. But into these we must plunge on some other occasion. (*AN*, 14–15)

James's formulation, which echoes Roderick's metaphor for the will as an abyss of abysses, acknowledges the peremptory logic of foreshortening that dictates Roderick's fall to be itself abysmal, for it casts the novel itself into the abyss of allegory. Although James defers our own plunge into the representational abyss glimpsed here, the novel's foreshortening strategy creates the effect of a "great lapse" like Roderick's "lapse of the mere 'inspired' state" (NY, 108).

James's association of Roderick's allegorical plunge with the novel's alleged structural problem makes it clear that the flaw in question in *Roderick Hudson* is not really the time scheme at all, but the allegorical turn that the novel takes midway with the introduction of Christina Light. James discovers that he has written an allegorical novel in spite of himself; he suffers from the same dilemma as Roderick. His remark in the preface that the novel's imperfection "stared me in the face" explicitly echoes Roderick's speech about his first unsuccessful statue: "It was bad from the first; it has fundamental vices. I have shuffled them in a measure out of sight, but I have not corrected them. I can't. . . . They stare me in the face" (*AN*, 12; 263). With characteristic inconsistency, James insists later in the preface that such "faults may show, faults may disfigure, and yet not upset the work" (*AN*, 15). To recall James's complaint about allegory in *Hawthorne,* the novel has nonetheless exposed its own machinery.

J. Hillis Miller formulates the problem of temporal discontinuity characteristic of the allegorical sign as the problem of a disjunction between material base and ideological superstructure, or between allegorical vehicle and tenor. Although allegory by its nature posits a continuous relation between narrative events and their allegorical meaning, the relation

between vehicle and tenor is not only arbitrary, but potentially disjunctive. As Miller concludes of Hawthorne's "The Minister's Black Veil":
"There is an apparently remediable division between material base, that
is, realistic story, and ideological superstructure, that is, allegorical meaning. The reading of the story has shown that this disjunction between
meaning and carrier of meaning may not be a remediable discrepancy
but an ineluctable necessity." This disjunction between vehicle and tenor
is not local or contingent, but a radical and universal feature of language
itself: "the first disjunction disappears within an even more radical separation, that between any sign whatsoever and a meaning that is not
momentarily absent, but wholly unreachable." [20]

This disjunction between realistic base and allegorical superstructure
is the focus of much of *Hawthorne,* for example James's complaint about
the incongruity between realistic "kernel" and allegorical "envelope" in
"The Bosom-Serpent." It is the lack of correspondence between "images" and "spiritual facts" (*LC,* I, 408) that accounts for the mechanical
character of certain of Hawthorne's fictions. The relation between vehicle and tenor is arbitrary rather than natural, mechanical rather than
organic. James's 1896 essay on Hawthorne, which expresses ambivalent
praise for Hawthorne's imaginative capacity to "deck out" his impoverished subject matter by assuming a "life of the spirit" in excess of his
"mere eye of sense," diagnoses a comparable allegorical disjunction between his chosen objects and the shadows they cast: "[Hawthorne's imag-
ination] ended by living in a world of things symbolic and allegoric, a
presentation of objects casting, in every case, far behind them a shadow
more curious and more amusing than the apparent figure" (*LC,* I, 459–
60).[21] Hawthorne's strength, however diminished here by the epithet
"fancy," is claimed to be the imaginative power—a kind of Jamesian
"going behind" ("It was a question of looking behind and beneath for
the suggestive idea")—exemplified by his ability to infer or impute multiple levels of signification to objects offered to the "mere eye of sense."
"Any figure therefore easily became with him an emblem, any story a

20. Miller, *Hawthorne and History,* 119.
21. It is important to keep in mind that James here uses the terms "symbolic" and
"allegoric" roughly synonymously, not with the Coleridgean distinction addressed above.

parable, any appearance a cover" (*LC,* I, 459, 460). Yet this very strength
is what opens Hawthorne to the disjunction between "shadow" and
"figure" (not, as the passage might lead us to expect, between shadow
and object) that is the hallmark of allegory.

This allegorical disjunction is, of course, a central concern of Hawthorne's own fiction. *The Marble Faun,* to confine ourselves to the example at hand, extensively theorizes the question of correspondence between allegorical sign and meaning. Sculpture exemplifies the problem
of investing "senseless stone" with "spiritual idea"; as Miriam remarks,
"I fancy it is still the ordinary habit with sculptors, first to finish their
group of statuary—in such development as the particular block of marble
will allow—and then to choose the subject; as John of Bologna did with
his 'Rape of the Sabines' " (272, 96). The allegorical superstructure is a
retrospective imposition that has no organic connection to the sculpture
it claims to interpret. Elsewhere, however, the narrator advances a theory
of sculpture as the uncovering of a figure already "imbedded in the
stone," freed from "its encumbering superfluities." According to this theory, the spiritual idea precedes its material incarnation, as when Miriam
examines "a half-finished bust, the features of which seemed to be strug-
gling out of the stone" (89). But this second theory of representation is
rendered ironic, in the same passage, by the disjunction between conception and realization. The liberation of the figure in stone is executed
not by the artist himself, but by his workmen: there is a permanent
disjunction between creative "word" and the "hands" that work its material realization. In the manner of James's complaint about the mechanical character of allegory, the sculptures are thus "not [the sculptor's]
work, but that of some nameless machine in human shape."

The Marble Faun's exploration of the link between senseless stone and
spiritual idea finally becomes an ironic reflection on the distance between
the two, and sculpture is made to stand for the condition of pure materiality unredeemed by spiritualization. Like the coldness which James
associates with Hawthornian allegory (*LC,* I, 339, 403, 405), sculpture
figures the cold disembodiment of allegory. By metonymic extension,
Kenyon himself becomes a "man of marble" whose art is pure form
without affect (295). Significantly, the "fatal fall" that kills Miriam's persecutor leaves him "stone dead" (127, 130): the model is rendered an

inanimate dead sculpture, the ultimate embodiment of pure materiality without spirit.[22] The novel's ideal of producing "sermons in stones" (115) is defeated by an irremediable fissure between stone and sermon, image and idea. Though, as is typical of Hawthorne, *The Marble Faun* interprets itself relentlessly, the link between the action and the narrator's interpretive commentary often seems artificial rather than substantial, an obtrusive allegorical imposition. Indeed, the status of such narratorial commentary is one of the interpretive cruxes of Hawthorne's fiction.

Roderick's artistic impasse is precisely that of a disjunction between image and word, between allegorical vehicle and tenor. His dilemma reverses Kenyon's; for whereas Kenyon's problem is that of imposing meaning or spirit on completed sculptures, Roderick is at no loss for abstract subjects or allegorical themes, but they remain mere words, lifeless names that resist translation into material form. (Miss Blanchard displays in a comic vein the syndrome of the "thorny" and obtrusive moral; as Roderick says, "In all Miss Blanchard's roses you may be sure there is a moral. . . . You can see it sticking out its head, and, if you go to smell the flower, it scratches your nose," 291.) Roderick's "lapse" of inspiration resembles what James identifies as *The Marble Faun*'s lapse into allegory: "The story straggles and wanders, is dropped and taken up again, and towards the close lapses into an almost fatal vagueness" (*LC*, I, 447). The abyss into which Roderick plunges is, in the text's own terms, the abyss of allegory. Of course, the trope of the abyss is itself a reminiscence of *The Marble Faun*, the text whose presence threatens to overwhelm James's—figured as Roderick's—claims to artistic autonomy. Further, Hawthorne himself associates the trope of an abyss or chasm with what he calls romance. In a letter to Fields, Hawthorne notes that "in writing a romance a man is always, or always ought to be, careening on the verge of a precipitous absurdity, and the skill lies in coming as close as possible, without actually tumbling over."[23] Hawthornian romance, like Jamesian

22.   Jonathan Auerbach's "Executing the Model: Painting, Sculpture, and Romance-Writing in Hawthorne's *The Marble Faun*," *English Literary History*, XLVII (1980), 103–20, contends that sculpture represents for Hawthorne an "allegorical mode" (107). Auerbach's account of the Model as "key intermediary between the animating idea and the fulfilled artistic creation" is relevant here.

23.   Quoted by F. O. Matthiessen in *American Renaissance: Art and Expression in the Age of Emerson and Whitman* (1941; rpr. New York, 1968), 294.

allegory, is associated with the danger of a fatal fall into a formal and epistemological abyss. Jonathan Auerbach correctly observes that James's view of romance is epistemological rather than generic; he defines it "not by its subject matter but by its uncertain subjectivity," [24] for example the epistemological instability of first-person narration figured as "the darkest abyss of romance" in the preface to *The Ambassadors* (*AN,* 320). Insofar as the problem of allegory is the problem of the sign per se, as Miller demonstrates, the dilemma staged in *Roderick Hudson* can by no means be left behind along with the early career anxieties it clearly reflects.

Roderick's fall marks the novel's simultaneous exorcism and internalization of Hawthorne. Although Roderick embodies the problems posed by Hawthornian allegory, his fall marks the novel's most dramatic swerve *toward* Hawthorne—namely its repetition of the central event of *The Marble Faun.* As James observes retrospectively of *The American,* "I had been plotting arch-romance without knowing it" (*AN,* 25). Roderick's fall is both a literal loss of foothold or standpoint and an allegorical enactment of the suicidal lack of *locus standi* aligned with allegory in the Trollope essay. It signifies the loss of the equilibrium James credits in his preface to the novel's deployment of Rowland as central consciousness, the "point of command" that, he claims, enables its plot to "hang together" (*AN,* 15).

James's ambivalence toward Hawthorne, and his consequent ambivalence toward *Roderick Hudson,* in no way amounts to a rejection of allegory *per se.* Many of James's later novels, such as *The Sacred Fount, The Ambassadors, The Wings of the Dove,* and *The Golden Bowl,* to confine ourselves to the most obvious examples, contain a self-consciously allegorical dimension, as their titles reflect. [25] James's avowed rejection of

---

24. Auerbach, *The Romance of Failure,* 127. If it is indeed the case, as Edgar Dryden suggests, that romance for James "is a sign for a certain form of interpretation or understanding that occurs when the writer through the process of revision becomes the reader of his own work" (*The Form of American Romance,* 114), this alignment of romance with the trope of the abyss is peculiarly appropriate to the enterprise of the critical prefaces.

25. Anesko observes: "Written in the very years that James was coming to professional maturity, the Hawthorne biography announces a point of departure—not from Hawthorne's literary influence, which indeed grew even more pervasive in James's work over the years—but from the pattern of Hawthorne's career as a writer. Hawthorne was, to James, 'the last specimen of the primitive type of the man of letters,' an artist whose

allegory in *Hawthorne,* written several years after *Roderick Hudson,* appears both a strategic assertion of autonomy and a defensive localization of the larger problem of representation signified by allegory in the de Manian sense. *Roderick Hudson* may therefore be read as an allegory of the principle that requires James's violation of his own strictures against allegory—or as an allegory of the law according to which a work of art depends for its existence on an involuntary blindness to its own way of being, "the 'law' of the degree in which the artist's energy fairly depends on his fallibility" (*AN,* 297). For as James's fiction testifies, all narratives are both allegorical and realistic. *The Princess Casamassima* is both an account of the anarchist movement in London and an allegory of the fatal cost of the Jamesian reflective center; *What Maisie Knew* a study of adolescence and an allegory of the fundamental unaccountability of figurative language; *Roderick Hudson* a study of American artists in Italy and an allegory of James's relation to Hawthorne; and so on. Perhaps in recognition of this doubleness, James speaks in *Hawthorne* of reading allegory as "seeing a story told as if it were another and a very different story" (*LC,* I, 366).

Roderick's fatal fall thus becomes the fortunate fall that distinguishes James from Hawthorne, staging Hawthorne's own fall as allegorical writer, even as it reintroduces Hawthorne in the form of allegory. It is evocative at once of James's reading of Hawthornian allegory as a fallen, mechanical, and derivative narrative mode, of Roderick's literal and figurative fall as allegorical artist, and of James's own repetition of Hawthorne in *Roderick Hudson.* This repetition is itself an allegory of poetic influence, for to exorcise a literary forefather is inevitably to memorialize him. We are reminded of Rowland's paradoxical injunction to himself after learning of Roderick's engagement: "Remember to forget Mary Garland" (239). To remember to forget something, however, is to inscribe it indelibly into one's memory. And as *Roderick Hudson* powerfully testifies, to remember to forget Hawthorne is to remember him with a vengeance. The novel could be said to dramatize James's account of himself, in a passage of *Hawthorne* that repeats the flower imagery aligned

---

creative life, beautiful but brief, effectively closed a chapter in the history of the profession of authorship" ("*Friction with the Market,*" 61).

with Hawthornian allegory, as attempting to forget the *Twice-Told Tales* in order to recover them in a new and defamiliarized light: "The writer of this sketch . . . has been trying to forget his familiarity with them, and ask himself what impression they would have made upon him at the time they appeared, in the first bloom of their freshness, and before the particular Hawthorne-quality, as it may be called, had become an established, a recognised and valued, fact" (*LC*, I, 361). No wonder James finds, on rereading *Roderick Hudson* on the occasion of the New York Edition, that it "point[s] almost too stern a moral" (*AN*, 12), echoing his own earlier formulation of the moral exemplified by Hawthorne himself: "he has the advantage of pointing a valuable moral. This moral is that the flower of art blooms only where the soil is deep, that it takes a great deal of history to produce a little literature, that it needs a complex social machinery to set a writer in motion." The moral pointed by Hawthorne is the double-edged moral of Roderick himself. On one hand, Hawthorne and Hudson exemplify what James prefers to experience as the disabling cultural poverty of America in the first half of the nineteenth century. On the other, both are "oppressed with the burden of antiquity in Europe" (*LC*, I, 320, 373), embarrassed by the riches of a tradition they can neither master not forget.

But James's diagnosis of this double handicap calls attention to itself as an allegorical meaning of his own invention, an ideological superstructure imposed by the respective narrators of *Hawthorne* and *Roderick Hudson*. Further, and tellingly, the valuable moral pointed by James's Hawthorne itself pointedly recalls the preface to *The Marble Faun*, where Hawthorne writes: "The author proposed to himself merely to write a fanciful story, evolving a thoughtful moral, and did not purpose attempting a portraiture of Italian manners and character." Despite this assertion, Hawthorne never identifies the moral his novel proposes to evolve, and the passage continues with the famous statement about writing romance in America: "It will be very long, I trust, before romance-writers may find congenial and easily handled themes, either in the annals of our stalwart republic, or in any characteristic and probable events of our individual lives. Romance and poetry, ivy, lichens, and wallflowers need ruin to make them grow" (vi). The moral of *The Marble Faun,* insofar as it has one, may be this perceived lack as dramatized by Hawthorne and James alike.

Roderick Hudson's own ambition to point a moral remains suspended by a disjunctive or at least indeterminate connection between fanciful story and thoughtful moral. If the putative moral of *Roderick Hudson* is that of the abysmal dangers of allegory, James's story seems rather to confirm the inevitability of repeating Roderick's plunge into the abyss. Like the uncanny reappearance of Miriam's persecutor as the dead Capuchin, James's relation to Roderick and Hawthorne alike appears one of "deadly iteration."[26] Surely this is the real moral of the story.

26.   Hawthorne, *The Marble Faun,* 141.

4

Pious Misrepresentation in *The Ambassadors*

[H]e has by this time *seen* too much, felt too much, to retrace his steps to his old standpoint. The distance that separates him from it is, measured by mere dates, of the slightest, but it is virtually ground that he has got forever behind him. He is conscious of his evolution; he likes it—wouldn't for the world not have had it; albeit that he fully sees how fatal, in a manner, it has been for him.

—*Notebooks*

James's preface to *The Ambassadors* famously proclaims the novel to be "quite the best, 'all round,' of my productions." Yet even as he praises the formal economy attributed to the novel's organic fruition from its germ—"the closeness with which the whole fits again into its germ"— the preface develops an affectively charged thematics of sacrifice, betrayal, and treachery that qualifies its overt celebration of the novel as a formal achievement. James's successful realization of the narrative possibilities latent in the novel's originary "essence," the anecdotal germ identified with Strether's speech to Little Bilham in Gloriani's garden, turns out to exact a "costly sacrifice" and "exquisite treachery" (*AN*, 309, 308, 318, 325). The novel's aesthetic triumph is intertwined with a representational economy of compensation and loss that is familiar from the critical prefaces, if discordant in an essay whose tone is largely one of appreciative self-discovery.

The preface's charged vocabulary of treachery and loss echoes responsively the novel's own central thematic, which figures Strether's final break with the Newsomes as a sacrifice, payment, or renunciation. As

94

James puts it in a notebook entry, "He has never really enjoyed—he has lived only for Duty and conscience—his conception of them; for pure appearances and daily tasks—lived for effort, for surrender, abstention, sacrifice" (*Notebooks,* 141). What the narrator terms the "inexorable logic" (242) of Strether's accountability for his shift of allegiance describes also the logic of displacement by which he pays vicariously for Chad's betrayal of Marie de Vionnet, in a chiastic reversal that effects a "change of position and of relation, for each" (229).[1] Strether's "betrayed . . . consciousness" (*Notebooks,* 548) both figures and is doubled by James's own recognition of the representational treacheries endemic to the art of fiction.

This undercurrent of doubt as to the formal perfection the preface overtly claims for *The Ambassadors* is registered negatively as a series of disclaimers:

> I recall then in this connexion no moment of subjective intermittence, never one of those alarms as for a suspected hollow beneath one's feet, a felt ingratitude in the scheme adopted, under which confidence fails and opportunity seems but to mock. (*AN,* 309)

> Never, positively, none the less, as the links multiplied, had I felt less stupid than for the determination of poor Strether's errand and for the apprehension of his issue. (*AN,* 315)

Despite these negative assertions of mastery, the preface concludes that any work of art ultimately and ineluctably betrays its putative origin. Contrary to his initial claim that *The Ambassadors* brings to fruition the possibilities latent in its germ, springing "straight[ ]" from its "dropped grain of suggestion," James concedes, "One would like, at such an hour as this, for critical license, to go into the matter of the noted inevitable deviation (from too fond an original vision) that the exquisite treachery even of the straightest execution may ever be trusted to inflict even on

---

1.   On chiasmus and narrative crossings in the novel, see Michael Seidel, *Exile and the Narrative Imagination* (New Haven, 1986). For a full-scale study of chiasmus in James, see Ralf Norrman, *The Insecure World of Henry James's Fiction: Intensity and Ambiguity* (London, 1982).

the most mature plan" (*AN*, 307, 325). Even the straightest execution, like the straight narrative march or path sought in *What Maisie Knew*, cannot verifiably ensure the perfect realization of the text's ostensibly extranarrative germ. The organic development of the germ is blocked by a turning or troping that disrupts the ideal passage from vision to execution; the etymology of "deviation" indeed carries a figure of turning, as from a designated road or path (*via*). As David Carroll observes, the germ detected in the critical prefaces is always already "wind-blown" or otherwise displaced from its putative origin, an echo or trace rather than an ultimate source or ground.[2] The incident alluded to in the preface and identified as the germ of *The Ambassadors*, William Dean Howells' exhortation to Jonathan Sturges ("Live all you can; it's a mistake not to") reported two years later by Sturges to James,[3] illustrates the necessarily displaced and mediated character even of the germ that may be said to have a "factual" experiential basis. James indeed warns us that seeking the origin of the germ—the origin of the origin, as it were—requires going "too far back, too far behind," and yields a multitude of germs rather than a single source ("they come from every quarter of heaven. . . . They accumulate, and we are always picking them over, selecting among them," *AN*, 43). Because the germ is available only retrospectively and only in its effects, it remains strictly undecidable whether James's identification of the germ is a "constative" discovery or unconcealing or, on the contrary, an analeptic positing or imposition.

By concluding with a concession that qualifies its own thesis, the preface exemplifies the process of deviation it describes, shifting from the initial assertion that the novel has unerringly realized its germ or essence to a recognition that any text betrays its putative germ. James calls attention to the preface's straying or deviation from its own ostensible narrative path: "I am moved to add after so much insistence on the scenic side of my labour that I have found the steps of re-perusal almost as much waylaid here by quite another style of effort" (*AN*, 325). This reversal of argument, along with the intertextual resonances we have noted between the novel and preface, suggests that a larger dynamic may be in question.

2. Carroll, *The Subject in Question*, 62.
3. Kaplan, *Henry James: The Imagination of Genius*, 404–405.

What kind of deviation is at stake in James's preface, and in what way does *The Ambassadors* exemplify it—or deviate from it, as the case may be?

As Julie Rivkin argues in her account of the novel's logic of supplementarity, Strether's ambassadorial mission uncovers a contradiction between "the fidelity Mrs. Newsome demands" and "the means she employs": "Literality is the linguistic form of fidelity; if language could be kept from deviating into figuration, if messages could suffer no change in transmission, then the ambassador's errand of restoration might succeed." Instead, the linguistic aberrations generated by the novel's logic of delegation and ambassadorship render Strether "the figure for the necessary figurative turns and errors that accompany all acts of exchange and representation."[4] To Rivkin's brilliant analysis of the novel's allegorization of this logic, I would add that *The Ambassadors* dramatizes the infidelity of representation specifically by means of Strether's status as reflective center. For Strether's task is doubly one of representation: he both represents Mrs. Newsome's interests and repeats this mediation in his formal capacity as reflective intelligence. The compositional system of Strether's "project[ed]" consciousness (*AN*, 317) parallels his deputed representation of Mrs. Newsome. But the novel's logic of delegation, to borrow Rivkin's formulation, condemns Strether's mission to deviation at the level of representational strategy as well as at the level of plot. His inadvertent deviation from his appointed task, figured as a "revolution" like

---

4. Rivkin, "The Logic of Delegation in *The Ambassadors*," 823. Porter similarly argues that Strether "interferes in the world on which he serves as a lens, for he is one of the 'ambassadors' whose mere presence in Chad's Paris operates ironically to redirect Chad's steps to America" (*Seeing and Being*, 125–26). On the linguistic and hermeneutic status of Strether's quest, see especially Louise K. Barnett, "Speech in *The Ambassadors*: Woollett and Paris as Linguistic Communities," *Novel: A Forum on Fiction*, XVI (1983), 215–29; Nicola Bradbury, *Henry James: The Later Novels* (Oxford, 1979), 36–71; Maud Ellmann, " 'The Intimate Difference': Power and Representation in *The Ambassadors*," in *Henry James: Fiction as History*, ed. Bell, 98–113; Daniel Mark Fogel, *Henry James and the Structure of the Romantic Imagination* (Baton Rouge, 1981), 20–48; William Greenslade, "The Power of Advertising: Chad Newsome and the Meaning of Paris in *The Ambassadors*," *English Literary History*, XLIX (1982), 99–122; Richard Salmon, "The Secret of the Spectacle: Epistemology and Commodity Display in *The Ambassadors*," *Henry James Review*, XIV (1993), 43–54; and Michael Wutz, "The Word and the Self in *The Ambassadors*," *Style*, XXV (1991), 89–103.

Hyacinth's "lively inward revolution" or Maisie's "moral revolution," marks a turn or non sequitur in the novel's narrative and causal line. Further, this turn is itself duplicated by the novel's deviation from the germ identified in James's notebook entries and from the synopsis written for Harper & Brothers in 1900. *The Ambassadors* both thematizes and exemplifies the problematic of deviation described in James's preface—a problematic that must be understood not as the result of artistic failure or unrealized intention, but as a phenomenon internal to narrative itself.

James contends that the novel's formal integrity results from its deliberate self-restriction to Strether's perspective. The reflector strategy enables James to profit aesthetically from the "recurrent breaks and resumptions" resulting from the novel's serial appearance in 1903: "I had made up my mind here regularly to exploit and enjoy these often rather rude jolts—having found, as I believed, an admirable way to it; yet every question of form and pressure, I easily remember, paled in the light of the major propriety, recognised as soon as really weighed; that of employing but one centre and keeping it all within my hero's compass" (*AN,* 317). The designation of Strether as central consciousness counters the decentering effect of serial publication, imparting a "large unity" to the whole (*AN,* 318) despite the disjunctive interruptions of serialization. But the novel's compositional law unsettles the rhetorical and epistemological coherence it would ensure, for Strether's consciousness is decentered from the start—not by serial publication, as James anticipates, but by the very premise of ambassadorship. For while *The Ambassadors* is plotted as an extended drama of "seeing,"[5] an epistemological quest structured around the "compass" of Strether's organizing consciousness, Strether finally sees "too much," as James remarks in his notes. The novel ends when it does, not because the narrative potential of its central consciousness has been exhausted, as in *The Princess Casamassima* or *The Wings of the Dove,* but because, as in *Roderick Hudson* and *What Maisie Knew,* Strether's compositional inventiveness gets out of control. His sustained act of seeing intervenes to the point of producing the very de-

---

5. Much has been written about pictorialism and impressionism in the novel; recent work on this topic includes Susan Griffin, *The Historical Eye: The Texture of the Visual in Late James,* 33–56, and Marianna Torgovnick, *The Visual Arts, Pictorialism, and the Novel* (Princeton, 1985), 174–86.

velopments it would preempt, and the representational strategy that designates him as ambassadorial central consciousness must finally sacrifice
him to its own "compositional law" (*AN,* 317). His intervention on Mrs.
Newsome's behalf exacerbates the interpersonal "tangle" it would remedy. Fatally unable to account for himself in either ethical or narrative
terms, Strether is sacrificed in a figurative expression of the novel's own
deviation from the origin sought in the preface.

We have seen that James figures the compositional law of *What Maisie
Knew* as a line connecting Maisie's knowledge to the third-person translation of the narrator's discourse, although this "straight march" is inevitably compromised by the figurative erring on which such translation
depends. *The Ambassadors* extensively revisits this system of linear imagery. Rivkin notes that Maria Gostrey's surname is suspended between
"go straight" and "go stray"; while Waymarsh, originally Waymark, conveys "the transformation of severity into uncertainty and the breakdown
of proper boundaries that is the fate of New England in the novel"; [6] it
further alludes to the conceptual "marsh" of his provincial philistinism.
Marie de Vionnet's surname is punningly close to "dévier," and
"Strether" puns conspicuously on "straight" and "straighter." He rumi-
nates over the question of Chad's "straightness," and explains that his
mission is to "take you straight home" (134, 103). Much as *What Maisie
Knew* seeks a straight narrative line that could be traced to the generating
source of Maisie's consciousness, so Strether aspires to follow a straight
path in his capacity as center of consciousness.

But Strether is condemned to deviation from the straight and narrow
by his "false position" as diagnosed in James's preface and notebook entry
(*AN,* 313): "He isn't straight, as it may be called, and he knows it"
(*Notebooks,* 561). He unwittingly becomes the "ground" and "pretext"
(227) of the interpersonal tangle he has been appointed to rectify:

> Strether felt, oddly enough, before these facts, freshly and consentingly
> passive; they again so rubbed it into him that the couple thus fixing his
> attention were intimate, that his intervention had absolutely aided and
> intensified their intimacy, and that in fine he must accept the consequence

6. Rivkin, "The Logic of Delegation in *The Ambassadors,*" 824.

of that. He had absolutely become . . . almost an added link and certainly
a common priceless ground for them to meet upon. (404)

Like Maisie, Strether is an "Ariachne" whose double agency conflates
the antithetical iconologies of Ariadne and Arachne. On the one hand,
he "mov[es] in a maze of mystic closed allusions" and "ke[eps] hold of
his thread" (198), promising to enforce the "straight remedy" (371) of
restoring Chad to Woollett and so save him from his labyrinthine erotic
liaison. On the other, he inadvertently compounds the "adverse tangle"
of the plot's ramifying "web" (*Notebooks*, 560, 248), even to the point of
potentially producing his own romantic liaison with Marie de Vionnet
(*Notebooks*, 558). In recognition of this danger, Strether initially begs off
from a second private meeting with her on the grounds that it would
not be "quite the straight thing" (183). The Harper's synopsis identifies
their final interview as the aesthetic and causal *telos* of the novel's linear
coherence or straight march; James notes, "I merely mark it with this
little cross as probably the most beautiful and interesting morsel in the
book. . . . It is really the climax . . . toward which the action marches
straight from the first" (*Notebooks*, 574). It is as if James imagines the
synopsis itself can guarantee the linear coherence of the (as yet) unwritten
novel; assuring the reader of a straight path through the narrative, the
postscript confidently asserts, "I have doubtless said a great deal more
than it may seem to you at first easy to find your way about in. The way
is really, however, very straight" (*Notebooks*, 576). But the cross with
which James marks the scene reinscribes the adulterous crossing or chiastic exchange it would preempt, namely the emergence of Strether's own
romantic interest in his charge's lover. The deviation figured in Marie de
Vionnet's name turns out to be inherent even to the straightest narrative
line. Despite James's insistence that no novel has ever "sprung straighter
from a dropped grain of suggestion" (*AN*, 307), the narrative ramifications Strether produces as reflective center cannot be predicted or naturalized in the manner suggested by James's characteristic organic imagery.

The text provides a tiny allegory for Strether's representational "betray[al]" of Mrs. Newsome (*Notebooks*, 548) in their correspondence,

which implicates him in a cycle of perpetual belatedness and unaccountability:

> Again and again as the days passed he had had a sense of the pertinence
> of communicating quickly with Woollett—communicating with a quick-
> ness with which telegraphy alone would rhyme; the fruit really of a fine
> fancy in him for keeping things straight, for the happy forestalment of
> error. (99)

> Certain it is at any rate that he now often brought himself balm by the
> question, with the rich consciousness of yesterday's letter, "Well, what can
> I do more than that—what can I do more than tell her everything?" (182)

> His message to Mrs. Newsome, in answer to her own, had consisted of
> the words: "Judge best to take another month, but with full appreciation
> of all reenforcements." He had added that he was writing, but he was of
> course always writing; it was a practice that continued, oddly enough, to
> relieve him, to make him come nearer than anything else to the con-
> sciousness of doing something. . . . Wasn't he writing against time, and
> mainly to show he was kind?—since it had quite become his habit not to
> like to read himself over. (236–37)

Although James would have it that the novel's rhetorical strategy is im-
mune to deviation from the compass of Strether's consciousness—the
preface refers to "the projection of his consciousness . . . without inter-
mission or deviation" (*AN,* 317)—Strether finds himself in a conundrum
that confounds straightness with error. As the synopsis notes, "The more,
at this point, everything grows, the more he tries, by letter, to keep her
in touch with it" (*Notebooks,* 561). But because each installment of Strether's narrative generates more discourse, more figurative language, it produces the very deviational erring it would correct. The "forestalment of
error" effected by the letters is itself a discursive temporizing, an errant
"writing against time" for which Strether is accountable. As a consequence, "the whole question of his regular report to Mrs. Newsome [is],
on the evidence before him, more and more difficult to meet" (*Notebooks,*
556). Each report creates the need for further explanatory narrative. His

"regular report" is faintly oxymoronic, since no narrative is regular in the etymological sense of being subject to an extranarrative rule or law—such as the law of organic development, simultaneously asserted and denied in James's preface, that assures a straight development from germ to whole. This situation is further compounded by the irony that Strether's correspondence with Mrs. Newsome is conspicuously absent from the narrative, an absence or hollow at the novel's center like the "suspected hollow beneath one's feet" which the preface confidently denies.

Strether's dilemma is doubled by James's recollection of his own narratorial belatedness vis-à-vis his reflector: "These things ["poor Strether's errand and . . . the apprehension of his issue"] continued to fall together . . . even while their commentator scratched his head about them; he easily sees now that they were always well in advance of him. As the case completed itself he had in fact, from a good way behind, to catch up with them, breathless and a little flurried, as he best could" (*AN*, 315). James's central intelligence ultimately resists representation altogether: "A whole process begins to take form in him which is of the core of the subject, and the steps and shades in the representation of which I cannot pretend here to adumbrate" (*Notebooks*, 560). As in *What Maisie Knew*, the first-person intrusion marks a deviation into the unrepresentable that calls into question Strether's *locus standi* as reflective center. But whereas the notebook entry emphasizes the impossibility of adumbrating the steps and shades of Strether's "evolution" (*Notebooks*, 568), the preface retrospectively affirms James's ability to represent it.

> What the "position" would infallibly be, and why, on his hands, it had turned "false"—these inductive steps could only be as rapid as they were distinct. I accounted for everything . . . by the view that he had come to Paris in some state of mind which was literally undergoing, as a result of new and unexpected assaults and infusions, a change almost from hour to hour. He had come with a view that might have been figured by a clear green liquid, say, in a neat glass phial; and the liquid, once poured into the open cup of *application*, once exposed to the action of another air, had begun to turn from green to red, or whatever, and might, for all he knew, be on its way to purple, to black, to yellow. (*AN*, 314)

Although Strether fails to account for his "assaults and infusions" as receptive intelligence, his false position furnishes the basis of James's own
triumphant accountability. Like the chemical troping of *What Maisie
Knew*, this passage figures a fatal turning, in the doubly chemical and
tropological sense, of the Jamesian receptive vessel. Its figuration rehearses
several familiar Jamesian tropes: the cup of experience from *The Portrait
of a Lady* and its transmutations through *The Sacred Fount* and *The Golden
Bowl*; the vessel or receptacle of the Jamesian center of consciousness;
and the chemical imagery associated with representation in the critical
prefaces. Strether's consciousness is figured as a chemical that changes
color when exposed to the air, a change or turn like the etymological
turn of his "revolution" (*Notebooks*, 142). (His transfer of allegiance to
Marie is called a "conversion" [233]—another "differential turning," as
Jonathan Arac notes.[7]) The passage further resonates curiously with the
famous speech urging Little Bilham to "live," in a figure suggestive of
the Jamesian receptive vessel itself: life, Strether says, is "a tin mould
. . . into which, a helpless jelly, one's consciousness is poured—so that
one 'takes' the form, as the great cook says, and is more or less compactly
held by it" (153).

In a turn or reversal like the exposure of Maisie's adulteration, Strether
is thus fatally compromised by what James figures as his "fermentation"
(*Notebooks*, 553). His turn of allegiance from Woollett to Paris is the
analogue of, and figure for, his unwitting misrepresentation as central
consciousness.[8] The "monstrosity" of which Chad had been accused de-
volves onto Strether himself, whose imagination is pronounced "monstrous" (94, 377). Whereas Chad is revealed to be a "cad" capable of
betraying Madame de Vionnet, it is Strether who—according to the
narrative logic that holds him accountable for the events he represents,
pays vicariously for this betrayal: "it was he somehow who finally paid,

7. Jonathan Arac, *Critical Genealogies: Historical Situations for Postmodern Literary Studies* (New York, 1987), 257.

8. For a deconstructively inflected reading of his renunciation as an "ethical turn"
that observes "the necessary illusion within language of ethical determination," see Myler
Wilkinson, "Henry James and the Ethical Moment," *Henry James Review*, XI (1990), 153–
75, 171.

and it was others who mainly partook. Yes, he should go to the scaffold yet for he wouldn't know quite whom" (337).

Strether's fundamental unaccountability brings the novel to a definitive representational impasse. As the synopsis observes, he has "*seen* too much, felt too much, to retrace his steps to his old standpoint" (*Notebooks,* 568). This loss of standpoint or *locus standi* results in a "queer displacement of his point of view," a "collapse" that figures the collapse of the novel's own point of view (292–93, 82, 125, 246). Like Roderick's great lapse, Strether's ensuing "lapse of life" (414) lands him in the abyss itself.

> It was as if he had found out he was tired . . . from that inward exercise which had known, on the whole, for three months, so little intermission. That was it—when once they were off he had dropped; this moreover was what he had dropped to, and now he was touching bottom. He was kept luxuriously quiet, soothed and amused by the consciousness of what he had found at the end of his descent. (383)

In short, he lands in the abyss of deviation and difference that is written into the novel's representational scheme. (As James notes in the synopsis, "he finds himself sinking . . . up to his middle in the Difference—difference from what he expected, difference in Chad, difference in everything," *Notebooks,* 561–62.) His "*volte-face*" (*Notebooks,* 142, 563) precipitates both this figurative fall and an "extinction" or virtual death:

> It amused him to say to himself that he might for all the world have been going to die—die resignedly; the scene was filled for him with so deep a death-bed hush, so melancholy a charm. That meant the postponement of everything else—which made so for the quiet lapse of life; and the postponement in especial of the reckoning to come—unless indeed the reckoning to come were to be one and the same thing with extinction. (414)

The price of the "imagination galore" ascribed to Strether as Jamesian reflector turns out to be monstrous, requiring the representational extinction or effacement thematized by his return to America. Although James's preface asserts that Strether's imagination "wouldn't have wrecked him," this is exactly what it *does* do, thus exposing the very "hollow beneath one's feet" whose existence the preface denies—namely, the dependence of James's own narrative *locus standi* on Strether's false position (*AN*, 310, 309, 313). This is the false position of the Jamesian center of consciousness itself, which is condemned to "pious misrepresentation" (*Notebooks*, 573).[9] The novel parodies this dilemma in Waymarsh, whose acquisitive "sacred rage" places him in a "false position" vis-à-vis Europe (340). (In an ironic and deflating replay of his speech to Little Bilham, Strether delivers this odd injunction to Waymarsh: "*Let* yourself, on the contrary, go—in all agreeable directions. These are precious hours—at our age they mayn't recur. Don't have it to say to yourself at Milrose, next winter, that you hadn't courage for them." And then as his comrade queerly stared: "Live up to Mrs. Pocock" [343]. One wonders of what living up to Mrs. Pocock would consist.)

James speaks of the propriety of confining the narrative to the compass of Strether's consciousness, much as Strether himself "has to keep in view proprieties much stiffer and more salutary than any our straight and credulous gape are likely to bring home to him" (*AN*, 321). Yet the charged imagery of the preface implicitly questions the propriety of the narrative principle that entails Strether's sacrifice: "a principle, we remember, essentially ravenous, without scruple and without mercy, appeased with no cheap nor easy nourishment. It enjoys the costly sacrifice and rejoices thereby in the very odour of difficulty" (*AN*, 318). The novel's fidelity to this principle secures the formal success the preface praises. But as it equally insists, the artist "sows his seed at the risk of too thick a crop" (*AN*, 312). The novel's germ or essence can neither be projected into the future nor analeptically recovered from the past. *The Ambassadors* cannot, any more than Strether himself, retrace its footsteps to its original standpoint. As the preface to *The Golden Bowl* avers, it is impossible to retrace one's footsteps without deviating from one's original path:

> It was, all sensibly, as if the clear matter being still there, even as a shining expanse of snow spread over a plain, my exploring tread, for application to it, had quite unlearned the old pace and found itself naturally falling

9. As Rivkin comments, Mrs. Newsome "can almost be seen as a parody of the absent author who 'works the whole thing out in advance' only to find the scheme revised in the act of execution" ("The Logic of Delegation in *The Ambassadors*," 824).

into another, which might sometimes indeed more or less agree with the original tracks, but might most often, or very nearly, break the surface in other places. What was thus predominantly interesting to note, at all events, was the high spontaneity of these deviations and differences, which became thus things not of choice, but of immediate and perfect necessity: necessity to the end of dealing with the quantities in question at all. (*AN,* 336)

Elsewhere in the preface, James speaks of the ethics of narrative artistry in terms of a turning or troping beyond the writer's choice or mastery: "I track my uncontrollable footsteps, right and left, after the fact, while they take their quick turn, even on stealthiest tiptoe, toward the point of view that, within the compass, will give me most instead of least to answer for" (*AN,* 328). This formulation figures the problem of answerability it describes. "Compass" is used here in the sense of range or scope, but also suggests a circle, circuit, circumference, enclosing line, or other boundary. Its implication of closure and unity appears incompatible with certain other details: with the uncontrollable footsteps by which this compass is said to have been reached, with the trope of turning which James aligns with the unpredictable trajectories of trope itself, and perhaps also with the passage's retrospective cast, which suggests that the closure James asserts here is a retrospective imposition. He can retrace his steps only metaleptically, after the fact, for example in the act of retrospective self-mastery undertaken in *The Art of the Novel.*

Rather than recover the novel's origin or ground, the preface to *The Ambassadors* uncovers the suspected hollow beneath one's feet whose existence James denies. Like Strether, who loses both his footing and his standing, despite his closing affirmation of a *locus standi* ("Then there we are!" [10]), the novel misplaces its narrative and epistemological standpoint, its *locus standi* or standing place. It enacts the very "subjective intermit-

---

10.   Meili Steele observes that the "metatextual gesture by which he seals his rhetorical victory does not close the text. (Indeed, Strether's line is a *mise en abyme* of the nineteenth-century narrator's gesture of closure)" ("Value and Subjectivity: The Dynamics of the Sentence in James's *The Ambassadors,*" 131). On the novel's closing line, see also Michael Levenson, *Modernism and the Fate of Individuality: Character and Novelistic Form from Conrad to Woolf* (Cambridge, U.K., 1991), 73–74; and Marianna Torgovnick, *Closure in the Novel* (Princeton, 1981).

tence" (*AN*, 309) whose occurrence James denies, namely the epistemological and rhetorical instability of the center of consciousness which
the narrative both veils and discloses. Its deviation from James's prospec-
tive and retrospective narratives (in the Harper & Brothers abstract and
critical preface) repeats Strether's own act of misrepresentation, and so
marks a difference internal to the novel itself. (For example, the abstract's
account of Mrs. Newsome as being deeply in love with Strether differs
sharply from the muted irony of the novel's treatment of her.) As the
preface to *The Spoils of Poynton* speculates, "where do we place the beginnings of the wrong or the right deviation?" (*AN*, 120). Our need to
distinguish the right from the wrong deviation, as when Strether avoids
being "wrong" by renouncing both Marie de Vionnet and Maria Gostrey, but with the equivocal reward of being "dreadfully right," as Maria
observes on the novel's final page (438), is at once imperative and impossible.[11]

Finally, James's recognition of his novel's "inevitable deviation" from
its ostensible origin enacts the very conundrum it would describe, for to
name a deviation as inevitable is surely to put in question its status as a
deviation: James's formulation deviates even from itself. Such deviance
may be our sole access to the origin, ground, or standing place James
seeks in *The Art of the Novel,* as the preface to *The Golden Bowl* makes
explicit: "The deviations and differences might of course not have broken
out at all, but from the moment they began so naturally to multiply they
became, as I say, my very terms of cognition" (*AN*, 337). *The Ambassadors*
diagnoses this state of affairs with undeviating rigor.

11.   A helpful analysis of the novel's troping on "right" is to be found in Levenson,
Modernism and the Fate of Individuality, 61–63.

5

Abysmal Consciousness in *The Wings of the Dove*

James's preface to *The Ambassadors* speculates that one measure of aesthetic mastery is the willful trying of the resources of narrative fiction, the "real extension, if successful, of the very terms and possibilities of representation and figuration" (*AN,* 319). Each of James's late triad—*The Ambassadors, The Wings of the Dove,* and *The Golden Bowl*—extravagantly extends the representational range of the novel. In *Wings,* the ex-centric or decentering effects that inhere in the Jamesian reflector are formalized into a compositional principle of shifting focalization or "successive centres"—a strategy of "merciful indirection" (*AN,* 296, 306) that circles the absent or elided center of Milly's consciousness.[1] Milly is seen at a double remove, through the indirection of Kate's and Densher's perspectives as well as the indirect discourse of the Jamesian reflector. In a formal and representational analogue of her death, Milly's narratorial perspective is gradually effaced and erased from the text altogether: as James explains, her case "ceases at a given moment to be 'renderable' in terms closer

---

1.   This displacement of the novel's formal center does not in itself jeopardize the reflector's posited status as narrative ground. Carroll notes, "A plurality of singular and well-defined points of view . . . is in principle acceptable [to James] if the various points of view can be made to focus on a subject" (*The Subject in Question,* 51). For Leo Bersani, "all the principal centers—first Kate, then Milly and finally Densher—seem to be reenacting the moral choice of the mind from whose point of view the story is really being enacted" (*A Future for Astyanax: Character and Desire in Literature* [New York, 1984], 142). On the causal relation between plotting and point of view, see Bersani's "The Narrator as Center in *The Wings of the Dove,*" *Modern Fiction Studies,* VI (1960), 131–44.

than those supplied by Kate's intelligence, or, in a richer degree, by Densher's" (*AN,* 301).

James conceives this scheme of successive centers of consciousness as promising narrative grounding and stability, yielding "sufficiently solid *blocks* of wrought material, squared to the sharp edge, as to have weight and mass and carrying power." This ideal of sculpturesque solidity appears the antidote to the loss of standpoint dramatized in *The Ambassadors.* But James recognizes it to have been only "my first and most blest illusion," for he is struck in retrospect by "the gaps and the lapses" of the completed novel (*AN,* 296). For the preface goes on to disparage the text's "misplaced pivot" (*AN,* 306), a formal imbalance that is said to create a "makeshift middle" and a "false and deformed" second half. Yet there may be a covert continuity between the narrative misplacement James diagnoses in the finished text and the "carrying power" he ascribes to his envisioned narrative blocks—a carrying evocative of the linguistic displacement or "carrying over" of metaphor itself. And in fact, what is disclosed by James's rereading of *Wings* is less a corrigible formal flaw than an "inveterate displacement of [the] general centre" (*AN,* 302), a decentering of the reflective center that is intrinsic rather than local.

The novel's representational strategy is indeed virtually one of "gaps" and "lapses." The preface notes that "the case prescribed for its central figure a sick young woman, at the whole course of whose disintegration and the whole ordeal of whose consciousness one would have quite honestly to assist" (*AN,* 289). The novel's sacrifice of its reflector, Milly Theale, is underlined by the text's ostentatious, if ironized, Christological strain. Kate and Densher attain a kind of authorial control over Milly's fate, for her elision from the narrative mirrors the success of their plot to secure her fortune. It is in this sense that *The Wings of the Dove* illustrates what Laurence Holland has called the analogy between form and tragedy in the novel. He notes that the narrative adopts a "rhythm of approach and withdrawal" that teasingly elides the representation of critical scenes, especially those pertaining to Milly's illness and death. Even as it pays "tribute" to Milly's triumph by drawing back from her final agony, Holland contends, James's text becomes complicit in what Densher (with the narrator's mediation) calls the "conspiracy of silence"

(388) that surrounds her. The novel's fragmented and aestheticized por-
trayal of Milly thus repeats her objectification at the level of plot, and
she is "betrayed by the very fiction that enshrines her"[2] in a complicitous
collusion between Kate's design and James's own.

While the narrative elides or circles the absent center of Milly's consciousness, she retains a ghostly causal and authorial power. The novel's
homology between form and theme is crucially linked to the reflector
method—a method which, like the representation of Milly herself, the
text both courts and evades. Although *The Wings of the Dove* renounces
the reflective center's claim to consistency of point of view, Milly retains
the reflector's causal power through her equivocal authorship of the
novel's plot. Further, the complicity of James's representational strategy
in Milly's objectification and effacement from the narrative is both qualified and compounded by the radically double-edged effect of Milly
herself. Like Maisie's, Milly's effect in the narrative she ambiguously
presides over is double, simultaneously redemptive and fatal, performative as well as reflective. The text itself appears to read Milly's equivocal bequest as a gesture of sacrifice that redeems Densher. But there
emerges a gap, abyss, or disjunction between this thematic organization
and the novel's causal structure, whose intervention in this thematic
scheme renders it ironic. Like Roderick, Milly is sacrificed to the novel's
representational requirements; but like Rowland, she authors an ambiguous triumph from it.

Milly's "stricken state" (*AN*, 294), the presumptive germ of the narrative, is not only unrepresented, but unrepresentable as such, approach-
able only in a series of infinitely decreasing increments. The preface states
that this representational scheme aspires to give equal treatment to the
novel's center and circumference, Milly and the other characters respectively. James figures the narrative as a movement from circumference to
center: "Preparatively and, as it were, yearningly—given the whole
ground—one began, in the event, with the outer ring, approaching the
centre thus by narrowing circumvallations" (*AN*, 294). This formulation
describes an asymptotic series of successively smaller increments that can
approach but never coincide with the center which is its goal. The novel's

2.   Holland, *The Expense of Vision*, 320, 321.

representational strategy is like an asymptotic curve that draws continuously closer to Milly, yet remains separated by a distance that continuously decreases but can never be crossed. Milly is "taken up with the unspoken,"[3] aligned with the unspeakable itself, and the novel's putative center is an elusive void or abyss that can be known only indirectly or figuratively.

Not only are key scenes of the novel rendered abstract, even ontologically suspect, by their retrospective presentation; but its central events, Milly's death and Kate's assignation with Densher, are elided altogether. James pointedly links these two episodes when he insists on the unspeakability of Milly's death: "Heaven forbid, we say to ourselves during almost the whole Venetian climax, heaven forbid we should 'know' anything more of our ravaged sister than Densher darkly pieces together, or than what Kate Croy pays, heroically, it must be owned, at the hour of her visit alone to Densher's lodging, for her superior handling and her dire profanation of" (*AN,* 301). The convoluted syntax of this sentence obscures, or points to the already obscure, logical and causal relation between its two elements. The sentence is an anacoluthon, a syntactical displacement or failure of sequence: James frustrates our expectation of a parallel structure between knowing "more of our ravaged sister" and knowing "what Kate Croy pays." It is unclear whether Kate's payment in Densher's lodging is logically and causally parallel to, or subordinate to, Densher's piecing together of knowledge about Milly. If "what Kate Croy pays" is parallel to "what Densher darkly pieces together," then the sentence implies that Kate's payment for Densher's participation in her scheme is itself an indirect knowing of Milly—a possibility that would ironically align Kate's payment to Milly's agency. In any case, the anacoluthic asymmetry of James's formulation points to the text's larger causal anacoluthon.

Kate and Densher's relations are indeed fatally altered by Milly's absent and indirect mediation. In a series of parallel ironies, Kate's substitution of Milly for herself as the object of Densher's courtship sets in motion a chain of substitutions that finally eludes Kate's narrative control. The defeat of Kate's plot is made possible ironically by the very "bargain" by

3.   Henry James, *The Wings of the Dove* (1902; New York, 1965), 126.

which Densher exacts the payment of Kate's assent to visit him in his rooms. In keeping with an obsessional thematics of naming and silence, in a novel whose unspeakable central events, sex and death, elude representation, Densher is definitively silenced by the very act of naming his price. The consummation of his affair with Kate itself marks the beginning of his "turn"—a key trope in the novel—from Kate to Milly. This turn, the reversal on which the entire novel turns, both exposes the instability or reversibility of its chief conceptual opposition, the distinction between truth and lie, and points to a larger non sequitur in the work as a whole—to a radical fissure or disjunction between knowledge and act, means and ends, cause and effect.

This causal confusion is evident in the novel's treatment of Milly's unnamed illness, which reactivates the Osmond plot of *The Portrait of a Lady* with Milly as a conflation of Ralph and Isabel, both dying heiress and marriageable heroine. Ralph's signature mannerism of keeping his hands in his pockets is reassigned to Densher, here the mark of his egregious "want of means" (44). While Milly's illness is even more pointedly spiritual and figurative in character than Ralph's,[4] it is notable mainly for its unspeakability, "the veto laid . . . on any mention, any cognition" of it (361). Its causal power is proportionate to its very repression and lack of specificity. In this it resembles Lionel Croy's "unspeakable" act (14)— the unidentified crime that has impoverished the family, and so furnishes the posited origin of Kate's financial motives in using Milly. And if Milly's unnamed illness is the plot's operative "obscure cause" (87), its narrative presentation makes it appear not so much the cause as the effect of her betrayal. As a dormant narrative device activated by Mark's disclosure of Densher's engagement, since it is this disclosure that precipitates her famous turn to the wall, Milly's illness is both the source of her compo-

---

4. As Peter Brooks notes, the very "desemanticization" of her illness "permits presentation of Milly's case as purely volitional, a pure struggle of the will to live" (*The Melodramatic Imagination: Balzac, Henry James, Melodrama, and the Mode of Excess* [New Haven, 1976], 183). See also Susan Mizruchi, *The Power of Historical Knowledge: Narrating the Past in Hawthorne, James, and Dreiser* (Princeton, 1988), 237, and Virginia C. Fowler, "Milly Theale's Malady of Self," *Novel: A Forum on Fiction,* XIV (1980), 57–74. On medical discourse in the novel, see Lawrence Rothfield, *Vital Signs: Medical Realism in Nineteenth-Century Fiction* (Princeton, 1992), 163–74.

sitional power as central consciousness and the ground of James's narrative. As the preface puts it, terminal illness is "the very shortest of all cuts to the interesting state," as well as the condition "that might most quicken . . . [the reflector's] consciousness of all relations" (*AN,* 289). On the one hand, Milly's illness is the basis of her narrative authority, a *locus standi* or "something firm to stand on" (154). On the other, her death is virtually caused by her status as center of consciousness, for her illness quickens her receptive consciousness to an ultimately fatal degree: "her doom was to live fast. It was queerly a question of the short run and the consciousness proportionately crowded" (106). Her stricken state does double duty as cause and effect in the novel's plot.

Milly's illness is itself a figure for the "rich, romantic, abysmal" state (74) in which Susan Stringham finds her by the "dizzy edge" (83) of an Alpine precipice:

> if the girl was deeply and recklessly meditating there, she was not meditating a jump; she was on the contrary, as she sat, much more in a state of uplifted and unlimited possession that had nothing to gain from violence. She was looking down on the kingdoms of the earth, and though indeed that of itself might well go to the brain, it wouldn't be with a view of renouncing them. Was she choosing among them, or did she want them all? (84)

Like so many moments in James, this passage is vertiginously double, hovering between a self-consciously portentous allusion to the temptation of Christ[5] and a facetious literalization of the abyss, the Jamesian master-trope for the unspeakable. As in *Roderick Hudson, The Ambassadors,* and *What Maisie Knew,* the abyss is aligned with the unspeakable and with a narrative fall into metaphysical instability. James's preface singles out as Milly's defining narrative interest this ideal susceptibility to the abysmal: "What one had discerned, at all events, from an early stage, was that a

---

5. On the Christological resonances of this passage, see Holland, *The Expense of Vision,* 296. Milton's dove brooding on the vast abyss is present here, as are Hilda's doves from *The Marble Faun,* an intertext addressed by Elissa Greenwald in " 'I and the Abyss': Transcendental Romance in *The Wings of the Dove,*" *Studies in the Novel,* XVIII (1986), 177–92.

young person so devoted and exposed, a creature with her security hanging so by a hair, couldn't but fall somehow into some abysmal trap" (*AN*, 293). She declares that she "want[s] abysses," and is later conscious "of being here on the edge of a great darkness" in her relations with Kate (123, 126).

Milly's perch over the abyss further figures the novel's own strategy of hanging fire on the edge of the unspeakable. The idiom "hanging fire" is a privileged locution in the novel. Its syntactical analogue is the dash, the textual marker that enables so much of the dialogue to hang in equivocal suspension. As Ned Lukacher observes, the expression "hang fire" derives from the early history of firearms, referring to a delay between ignition and firing: to hang fire "is thus to be on the threshold between firing and not firing, in the interval between speech and silence."[6] The plot itself hangs fire in a state of sustained thresholding. A notebook entry speaks of Milly as being "on the threshold of . . . life" (*Notebooks*, 102); "The Doctor's Door," Alvin Langdon Coburn's frontispiece to the New York Edition, plays on this threshold motif. Much as Milly's tenuous narrative existence as absent center is drawn out by her temporizing on the threshold of the abyss, so the success of Densher's plot to fill his "abysmal need" of Kate depends on their ability to "play a waiting game" with Aunt Maud (69, 61).

Milly's encounter with an abysmal otherness at the edge of the precipice is repeated by her confrontation with the Bronzino portrait.

> Perhaps it was her tears that made it just then so strange and fair—as wonderful as he had said: the face of a young woman, all magnificently drawn, down to the hands, and magnificently dressed; a face almost livid in hue, yet handsome in sadness and crowned with a mass of hair rolled back and high, that must, before fading with time, have had a family resemblance to her own. . . . And she was dead, dead, dead. Milly recognized her exactly in words that had nothing to do with her. "I shall never be better than this." (144)

"It's down to the very hands," said Lord Mark.

6. Ned Lukacher, *Primal Scenes: Literature, Philosophy, Psychoanalysis* (Ithaca, 1986), 131.

"Her hands are large," Milly went on, "but mine are larger. Mine are huge."

"Oh, you go her, all round, 'one better'—which is just what I said. But you're a pair." (145)

This episode offers a proleptic microcosm of the entire novel; James's enigmatic reference in the preface to the "whole actual centre of the work, resting on a misplaced pivot and lodged in Book Fifth" may well allude to the Bronzino episode (*AN*, 306). The portrait's resemblance to Milly "down to the hands" links it to the "handling" and "manipulation" associated especially with Kate and Maud. Kate assures Densher he will "have a free hand" in his courtship of Milly, and his agreement to "make up to" her is figured as his dropping of Kate's hands to take hold of Milly's. Milly's large hands mark her as another manipulator, her triumphant manipulation being her bequest to Densher of both her money and her ineffaceable image: her unread letter to Densher is accordingly termed "the unrevealed work of her hand" (343, 258, 445).

The Bronzino is a richly overdetermined figure whose multiple suggestiveness links the two plots—Milly's illness and Kate's and Densher's surreptitious liaison—that are so obliquely yet insistently aligned in the preface. Lord Mark declares that Milly and the Bronzino are "a pair," foreshadowing Kate's pronouncement—itself ironically prophetic of her ultimate displacement by Milly in Densher's imagination—that Milly and Densher are "a pair" by virtue of their common victimization by her own plotting (237). Kate is repeatedly figured as a painting come to life (52, 113), and the Bronzino's metaphoric allusion to the novel's adulterous triangle is further underlined by an unspoken contextual detail: Bronzino's *Lucretia Panciatichi,* the portrait commonly assumed to be the one James has in mind, bears the inscription "AMOUR DURE SANS FIN"—an ironic gloss for the plot by which one "eternal love" displaces another.[7] Further, the Bronzino coercively figures Milly's future self: a valuable but immobile and posthumous image, like the "circle of eminent contemporaries, photographed, engraved, signatured, and in particular framed

---

7. John Carlos Rowe makes this point in *Henry Adams and Henry James: The Emergence of a Modern Consciousness* (Ithaca, 1976), 187.

and glazed," which Milly studies on the walls of Sir Luke Strett's office (155). Her turning of her face to the wall is indeed an odd concretization or literalization of her turn toward the "pale personage on the wall" (147) in this scene.[8] The swoon precipitated by her confrontation with the Bronzino is a proleptic loss of consciousness that foreshadows both her death and her deathlike effacement as center of consciousness.

Moshe Ron's essay on the motif of the portrait in James argues that it is the nature of a portrait to annihilate its subject or rob it of its essence.[9] The Bronzino conspicuously activates the "obscure cause" (87) of Milly's unspeakable disease: like Freud's uncanny, the portrait is a harbinger of death,[10] effecting an uncanny turn or reversal that identifies Milly with a dead double. Her vision of the Bronzino is a gaze into death's face, to invoke a key word that recurs in such idioms as "facing it," "facing the music," "taking it full in the face," "look it in the face," "the two faces of the question," "face-to-face," and "on the face of it." Like the abyss, "facing it" figures a confrontation with an unspeakable or annihilating otherness.[11] Milly's final gesture of turning her face to the wall is the ultimate self-effacement, parodied by Lionel Croy's sardonic offer to Kate to "efface" himself with "the final fatal sponge" (16)—an offer actualized by his abrupt disappearance from the novel.

8. On the Bronzino scene, see especially Brooks, *The Melodramatic Imagination*, 182–84; Nicola Bradbury, *Henry James: The Later Novels* (Oxford, 1979), 97–100, and " 'Nothing that is not there and the nothing that is': The Celebration of Absence in *The Wings of the Dove*," in *Henry James: Fiction as History*, ed. Bell, 82–97; Cameron, *Thinking in Henry James*, 126–30; Marcia Ian, "The Elaboration of Privacy in *The Wings of the Dove*," *English Literary History*, LI (1984), 107–36; and Lee Clark Mitchell, "The Sustaining Duplicities of *The Wings of the Dove*, *Texas Studies in Literature and Language*, XXIX (1987), 187–214, to whose discussion of causality in the novel I am indebted. Jonathan Freedman observes that the Bronzino scene rewrites the Pre-Raphaelite *topos* of confrontation with an image of a dead woman: "What initially appears to be a moment of existential self-discovery actually turns out to be a moment of specular doubling, a moment in which Milly constructs her 'self' in imitation of an aesthetic icon, an artistic Other" (*Professions of Taste: Henry James, British Aestheticism, and Commodity Culture* [Stanford, 1990], 214).

9. Moshe Ron, "The Art of the Portrait According to James," *Yale French Studies*, LXIX (1985), 222–37, 229–30.

10. Sigmund Freud, "The Uncanny," in *The Standard Edition of the Complete Psychological Works of Sigmund Freud*, trans. James Strachey (24 vols.; London, 1953–74), XVII, 218–53.

11. See J. Hillis Miller's essay by this title, "Facing It: James's 'The Last of the Valerii,' " in *Versions of Pygmalion*, 211–43.

In connection with this insistent face imagery, the portrait also evokes the trope of prosopopoeia, which projects a face onto the absent, dead, or inanimate. As J. Hillis Miller has put it, prosopopoeia is "haunted by death," a retrospective and compensatory covering over of a loss or break in sequence of which death is the proper name.[12] The loss of consciousness marked by Milly's swoon, a prolepsis of death, is such a break in sequence. The portrait is a kind of prosopopoeia in reverse that, like Freud's uncanny, dooms her by the very act of representing her as a "dead" art object. By thematizing the trope of prosopopoeia, further, the portrait implicitly comments on the novel's representational strategy. The Jamesian reflector is a form of prosopopoeia that attributes a human consciousness to a rhetorical construct, yet also defaces or effaces its reflector through the rhetorical self-dismantling traced here. The novel indeed develops a sustained connection between the motifs of the portrait and of the mirror—as in Kate's gaze into the mirror in the opening passage—the traditional trope of mimesis and recurring Jamesian trope for the reflector. If to "face it" is to encounter an unspeakable otherness, to efface oneself is to place oneself beyond the pale of representation—for example in the blank space between Books Eight and Nine that marks Kate's assignation with Densher, or the virtual absence from which Milly exerts her odd power.

Although Milly's turning her face to the wall is typically read as a renunciation that redeems Kate and Densher, this equivocal "act of renouncement" (413) actually produces the definitive break between them, surpassing their own design in its consequences. There emerges a disjunction between the novel's thematic organization, which assigns Milly a Christological role through her renunciation and redemption of Densher, and the structure of causation that enables her to author the permanent division between Kate and Densher. She bestows the "blessing and a cheque" (209) they had hoped to receive from Aunt Maud, but with ironic results. Her renunciation is equally a "trap" (251), and its consequences are less beatific than abysmal. She is equivocally figured as "a survivor of a general wreck" (158), "a creature saved from a shipwreck" (229–30), yet also, in James's preface, as a seductive siren who

12. Miller, *Versions of Pygmalion*, 48, 74.

lures others to wreckage: "entangled and coerced," they are "drawn in as by some pool of a Lorelei . . . terrified and tempted and charmed; bribed away, it may even be, from more prescribed and natural orbits" (*AN,* 291). Milly appears here an aquatic incarnation of Maisie, enmeshing others in a labyrinthine tangle of narrative complications (70, 123, 382). The passage continues: "I have named the Rhine-maiden, but our young friend's existence would create rather, all round her, very much that whirlpool movement of the waters produced by the sinking of a big vessel or the failure of a great business; when we figure to ourselves the strong narrowing eddies, the immense force of suction, the general engulfment that, for any neighbouring object, makes immersion inevitable" (*AN,* 293). In an inversion of his characteristic trope, the Jamesian vessel of consciousness here becomes the agent of catastrophic shipwreck. The novel itself figures Milly "stir[ring] the stream like a leviathan" (76), and her effect on Densher is likened to a "current . . . that, but for the absurdity of comparing the very small with the very great, he would freely have likened to the rapids of Niagara" (247–48). The Jamesian vessel of consciousness is here remarkable not for its vulnerability to a fatal overflowing of sensibility, but for its power to draw others into an abysmal engulfment.

Like the Lorelei whose effect is felt rather than seen, Milly's ultimate power over Densher is proportionate to her absence. The crisis that follows his last represented interview with Milly is a "turn" (357) that figures a chiastic turn or reversal beyond Densher's control. As a result of his unwitting turn from Kate to Milly, Milly becomes the referent alike of his action and of his inaction; from here on, Densher's actions refer ineluctably to her invisible but coercive agency. His last scenes with Kate revolve around the unspeakability of his final "face-to-face" (406) interview with Milly, itself elided in the narrative. Their relation is doomed to a perpetual deferral of this naming, a hanging fire over the "it" that now separates them. This "it" is forever beyond their reach, because Milly's final and crucial act coincides with her effacement from the narrative. Like Maisie, who cannot be worked into the novel's interpersonal system, Milly "exceeded, escaped" the "measure" (79) of logic and causality. She becomes unknowable at the very moment of her "act of renouncement." In a narratological expression of this renunciation, the

narrator himself withdraws altogether from her consciousness after Book
Nine. The center of consciousness is itself renounced, and the novel's
ethical crux remains a blank, an ellipsis that denies us any knowledge or
understanding of its grounds. Even after Milly's elision from the narrative,
her terrorizing viewpoint (as Kate says of Aunt Maud, 318) exerts a
ghostly coercive power as absent center of consciousness.

This coercion is the implication of a critical passage in chapter 32 that
simultaneously asserts and denies Densher's discovery of "the truth that
was the truest" about Milly.

> He had not only never been near the facts of her condition—which had
> been such a blessing for him; he had not only, with all the world, hovered
> outside an impenetrable ring fence, within which there reigned a kind of
> expensive vagueness. . . . It was a conspiracy of silence, as the *cliché* went,
> to which no one had made an exception, the great smudge of mortality
> across the picture, the shadow of pain and horror, finding in no quarter a
> surface of spirit or of speech that consented to reflect it. (388)

This passage is most remarkable for what it withholds: in imitation of its
theme of circling around an impenetrable truth, the passage circles and
evades identification of the truth about Milly it would name. Densher's
hovering around the impenetrable ring echoes with the preface's descrip-
tion of circling around Milly's consciousness in narrowing circumvallations. Further, the "great smudge of mortality across the picture" is an
oblique evocation of the Bronzino, conflating the tropes of the painting
and of the Jamesian reflector: Milly becomes, at once, a painting made
unreadable by a smudge or shadow and a reflective center that has ceased
to reflect. The "conspiracy of silence" Densher imputes to Milly's inti-
mates thus describes the novel's own representational strategy, which
elides her reflecting consciousness after Book Nine. Though the passage
claims that Densher is "in presence of the truth that was the truest about
Milly," it performatively testifies instead to her radical unreadability. If
Milly is surrounded in the text by a zone of narrative preterition, the
preface further asserts that death per definition resists representation: "the
way grew straight from the moment one recognised that the poet essentially *can't* be concerned with the act of dying" (*AN*, 289). We have seen

that the image of a straight line is a favorite Jamesian trope for the coherent narrative and causal linearity associated (as in *What Maisie Knew*) with the scenic method. Here, the straight path is provided instead by the representational elision of Milly's consciousness.[13]

Milly's death thus marks a break or lapse in continuity that can only be known by a catachrestic positing. As J. Hillis Miller writes: "Death is perhaps the most radical name, though still only one figurative name among others, for the intermittences that break the continuity of human life all along the line. Of those blank places nothing can be known directly. They can be named only in trope. The misreading of a similarity as an identity is a way of filling in that gap. The mistake gives the chasm of death a face, a figure, a name, and a spurious intelligibility."[14] The abyss is James's characteristic trope for this gap or chasm, which can be only partially crossed by the asymptotic movement described in the preface and in the passage just quoted. In his essay "How to Read?," Tzvetan Todorov figures reading as an "asymptotic activity" whose impossible goal is, "with the help of language, to grasp the work as pure difference," though difference cannot be grasped as such: "The task of a reading always consists, to a greater or lesser degree, not in obliterating difference, but in taking it apart, in presenting it as an *effect of difference* whose functioning can be known."[15] The analogue or dramatization of Milly's effacement from the narrative is Kate's destruction of the unread letter, token of the unspeakable knowledge that will forever separate her from Densher, "the knowledge of each other that they couldn't undo" (447). Densher's stipulation that the letter's terms "must remain—pardon my making the point—between you and me" (444) is ironically actualized: the letter, like Milly herself, definitively interposes between them. (In

13. James's "straight way" oddly evokes the "ideal straightness" (251) of Kate and Densher's design. Indeed, James uses the terms "game" and "design"—the novel's recurring terms for Kate and Densher's scheme—to refer to his own narrative artistry (*AN*, 305, 292).

14. Miller, *Versions of Pygmalion*, 125; see also 70–71, 74. In a discussion suggestive for the question of allegory, Greenwald contends that James attempts to repair the "gap" diagnosed in Hawthorne's writing "between symbols and what they represent"; but the novel can manifest "spirit" only in its gaps and absences (" 'I and the Abyss': Transcendental Romance in *The Wings of the Dove*," 177, 179).

15. Tzvetan Todorov, *The Poetics of Prose*, trans. Richard Howard (Ithaca, 1977), 237.

James's notebook, they "break" and Kate takes the money—a resolution already implicit in the text as we have it [*Notebooks*, 106]). By throwing the letter into the fire, Kate consigns it to perpetual unspeakability, to a threshold state or hanging fire between speech and silence.[16] Much like Fanny Assingham's smashing of the golden bowl, Kate's destruction of the unread letter ironically preserves its power forever to interpose between herself and Densher.

The burning of the letter marks Densher's definitive loss of what the narrator calls "the turn [Milly] would have given her act" (450). The turn inscribed in her unread letter is blank or illegible, beyond the reach of logic. It can neither be textually located nor logically explained, least of all by the knowledge from which it appears to follow, namely Lord Mark's disclosure of the secret engagement. Milly's renunciation itself remains unreadable and unknowable. Its representational analogue is the conspiracy of silence that denies us ultimate access to Densher's, Kate's, and Milly's consciousness alike. Like Milly's renunciatory bequest, Densher's final turn to her memory is alogical. Each of these events marks a break or lapse in the novel's causal logic, breaking with the chain of events from which it seems to follow and producing unpredictable effects in its turn.

Densher's turn to Milly appears less a motivated act than an effect of tropological turning beyond his control, a rhetorical slippage that actualizes the "lie"—a key word in the novel—of his courtship of Milly. The narrator's characterization of Lionel Croy as dealing out lies like the cards from a greasy old pack (7–8) is a figure for Kate and Densher's own game, whose success depends on the efficacy of two lies in particular: Kate's assurance to Milly that she has herself rejected him, and the lie of omission concealing the engagement. Aunt Maud's admonition to Densher that "I depend upon you now to make me right!" (240) by acting on her lie to Milly alludes to the slippage whereby his lie is performatively fulfilled when Milly supplants Kate in his imagination. In a sense, the novel turns on the question of at what point Densher begins to act out

16. As Lukacher notes in his reading of *The Turn of the Screw*, fire embodies a play of absence and presence, or of concealment and disclosure, that renders it an image of self-consuming and destructive knowledge (*Primal Scenes*, 129–32).

Kate's false report of him as being in love with Milly: as D. A. Miller observes, "Worldly masters tend to ignore the force of the context in which they operate, and hence the extent to which signifiers can produce their conventionally given signifieds in those who would wield them." [17] Much as Densher's lie about Milly becomes truth, so his silence about the secret engagement becomes performative by canceling it out. Densher recognizes this performative dimension of the lie when he tells Kate that if he had denied their engagement to Milly, he would have "stuck to it." Kate retorts, "you would have broken with me to make your denial a truth?" (404). Unknown to Densher, this in effect has already occurred. Ironically, his break with Kate is figuratively effected by their assignation itself, which decisively reverses the place of the two women in Densher's mind. Although afterward it seems that "Kate was *all* in his poor rooms, and not a ghost of her left for the grander" (349), it is Kate herself who is relegated to the status of a ghost forever dead to Densher. Indeed, in a reminiscence of Milly's swoon in the Bronzino scene, "Kate's presence affected him suddenly as having swooned or trembled away" (377). Milly may become the framed and glazed image figured by the Bronzino, but it is Kate whose presence dies to Densher, a ghostly unreality displaced by Milly's memory.

Densher's turn to Milly is precipitated by the very act of naming the price of his cooperation with Kate's plan. In violation of the "law of silence" (369) surrounding the engagement, Kate brings the unspeakable into the open by forcing Densher to name his terms: "If you want things named, you must name them." . . . "Since she's to die I'm to marry her?" . . . "To marry her." . . . "So that when her death has taken place I shall in the natural course have money?" . . . "You'll in the natural course have money. We shall in the natural course be free" (342–43). But Densher's desire to "bring his mistress to terms" belies the fatal vulgarity—the ultimate fallen term in James—of the act of naming them ("in love, the names of things, the verbal terms of intercourse were, compared with love itself, vulgar," 199–200). By naming his terms, Densher irrevocably alters them; indeed his final rupture with Kate is formulated as "the

---

17. D. A. Miller, *Narrative and Its Discontents: Problems of Closure in the Traditional Novel* (Princeton, 1981), 255.

difference . . . between their actual terms and their other terms" (451). Conversely, to articulate the "horrors" of Milly's death would be to "repudiate" Kate and Densher's consummation, "everything that, in Venice, had passed between them" (399). Yet Densher's silence equally effects this repudiation.

In a similar contradiction, Kate and Densher's scheme is figured simultaneously as a straight path and as a circling or deviation. Kate urges Densher to "go straight" (237) by courting Milly, but this straightforward tactic is incompatible with her "roundabout" design (246) of indefinite deviation and deferral, the strategy of indefinite temporizing in hope of securing Maud's eventual favor and financial backing. The devious, roundabout logic of their scheme ultimately makes it impossible for Densher to be straight with Kate herself. In response to his plea that they admit the failure of their plan, Kate consents in return for "an idea straight *from* you, I mean as your own" (420–21). But this Densher cannot produce, for in a catastrophic overfulfillment of Kate's idea, their relation is now ineluctably mediated by Milly. Kate's creation of the erotic triangle introduces a logic of mediation and substitution that finally eludes her control. The temporary substitution of Milly for herself as the object of Densher's courtship ironically facilitates his ultimate turn to Milly. Thanks to the triangular structure that routes desire through Milly, Densher has no straight ideas untouched by her mediation.

Densher's turn is one of a series of Jamesian cruxes figured as turns: Christopher Newman's belated turn to the fire in *The American*, Isabel Archer's final turn from Goodwood back to Osmond in *The Portrait of a Lady* ("She had not known where to turn; but she knew now. There was a very straight path"),[18] the multiple reversals of *The Turn of the Screw*, the unexpected "turn" taken by the outing that leads Charlotte and Amerigo to the golden bowl. At stake in each case is a turn or troping that resists narrative accountability. The figure of turning pervades *Wings*, recurring in such expressions as "turn the tables," "turn about," "turn the other cheek," "turn a corner," and the familiar Jamesian locution "turn it over." The novel's major plot developments are also figured as turns: the

18. Henry James, *The Portrait of a Lady*, ed. Nicola Bradbury (1881; Oxford, 1985), 644.

"blessed turn" of Aunt Maud's forbearance from asking Densher for a promise to leave Kate alone (66), the "useful ill turn" Kate's sister is inclined to do Densher (133), Densher's apprehension of Milly's decline as a "turn[ ] to the dismal" (362), and the final "tragic turn" of her health (411). This problematic of turning or troping is figured in *Wings* especially by the figure of chiasmus, as when Densher's demand, "Do you love me, love me, love me?" elicits this reaction from Kate: "Her surrender was her response, her response her surrender" (207–208). The chiastic formulation reflects the susceptibility of their relation to the reversal by which Milly supplants Kate in Densher's imagination in what the narrator calls "the queer turn of their affair" (412, 417). The words "perversity" and "version," which figure importantly in the Bronzino episode, inhabit the same etymological field and so extend this imagery of turning. Milly's confrontation with the portrait is pointedly aligned with her repeated vision of Kate through the "perverse" mediation of what she imagines as Densher's perception of her.[19]

A key Jamesian "turn" that may shed light on the problematic of turning in *The Wings of the Dove* is Christopher Newman's turn toward the fire after his burning of the document revealing the Bellegardes' murderous past—an action that clearly resonates with the fate of Milly's letter. Newman's turn to the fire to recover the paper is too late, much as Densher "start[s]—but only half—as if to undo [Kate's] action" (445). In the 1877 text of *The American*, Newman "instinctively turned to see if the little paper was in fact consumed; but there was nothing left of it." His turn is prompted by Mrs. Tristram's shrewd divination that the Bellegardes understand Newman to be incapable of blackmail: "Their confidence . . . was in your remarkable good nature! You see they were right."[20] In the text's double bind, Newman has proven himself a gentleman and worthy of the Bellegardes' daughter only at the price of renouncing her. But if it is indeed "instinctive," then his gesture belies the "good nature" his renunciation would seem to have demonstrated.

19.   On issues of mediation and triangulation here and elsewhere in the novel, see Eve Kosofsky Sedgwick's remarkable reading in *Tendencies* (Durham, N.C., 1993), 73–103, which traces a series of gender bifurcations in the novel produced by the homophobic silence surrounding Lionel Croy's unspeakable homosexuality.

20.   James, *Novels 1871–1880*, 871–72.

James excises the turn to the fire from the 1907 New York Edition, a revision that Sharon Cameron construes as implying instead his turn *away* from the fire (though the narrator is not, in fact, explicit about this).[21] Elsewhere in the 1907 text, however, the figure of turning is preserved: when Newman decides not to denounce the Bellegardes to the Duchess, he "seem[s] morally to have turned a high somersault and to find things looking differently in consequence."[22] In short, both Newman's renunciation of revenge *and* his impulsive turn to the fire are figured as "turns." If the alternative to a turn is a turn, it would seem that there is no escaping the symptomatic final turn of James's fictions.

A second figure for the causal structure of *Wings* appears in the recurring linguistic metaphor of the "broken sentence." The fate of Kate's impecunious family is figured as a "phrase . . . that dropped first into words, into notes, without sense, and then, hanging unfinished, into no words, no notes at all. . . . She hadn't given up yet, and the broken sentence, if she was the last word, *would* end with a sort of meaning" (6–7). "Broken sentence" describes much of the novel's dialogue, which hangs fire in a series of exclamations, ellipses, and unfinished questions. Broken sentence further names the trope of anacoluthon, whose grammatical or syntactical displacement here points to a larger failure of narrative continuity or causal sequence.[23] It identifies the lapse or failure of sequence that problematizes the relation between means and ends, or cause and effect. The novel's most prominent anacoluthon is Densher's turn to Milly, the anacoluthic event for which there is no causal or thematic preparation and that cannot be located at any one point in the text. His turn cannot be explained in psychological, characterological, or otherwise logical terms; it appears the "merely" rhetorical consequence of the infidelity of language to itself.

The possibility that Densher's act is a linguistic turn or troping beyond

21. Cameron, *Thinking in Henry James*, 39–40. She astutely connects this problematic of Newman's turn to the preface's discussion of romance, which aligns power with reversibility of position ("the 'power' of bad people that good get into, or *vice versa*").

22. Henry James, *The American* (1907; rpr. New York, 1936), 507, 533, Vol. II of *The Novels and Tales of Henry James*.

23. On anacoluthon, see J. Hillis Miller, "Ariachne's Broken Woof," *Georgia Review*, XXXI (1977), 44–60.

his control is the burden of the novel's last chapters, which worry obsessively over whether his relation to Milly has a basis or footing in the sense of a causal or metaphysical ground. He finds himself on a "false footing" (245) that threatens him with a fall into the abyss itself: "He was walking, in short, on a high ridge, steep down on either side, where the proprieties—once he could face at all remaining there—reduced themselves to his keeping his head" (310). In an image that recalls the Bronzino, this sense of an imminent fall is figured as a picture in danger of falling: "He felt himself . . . shut up to a room, on the wall of which something precious was too precariously hung. A false step would bring it down, and it must hang as long as possible" (358). Densher's dilemma plays out the panoply of figures aligned with the representational impasse of the Jamesian reflector, for example, the snapping of a cord or rope: "He was mixed up in her fate, or her fate, if that were better, was mixed up in *him,* so that a single false motion might, either way, snap the coil" (358).

In a reminiscence of Maisie's "jerk" and "slip from a foothold" after the exposure of her lack of a moral sense, Densher "[gives] a jerk round" (379) when Susan reveals that Lord Mark has told Milly of the engagement. Like Kate's "jerking" of Milly's unread letter into the flame (445), this jerk figures a fall or slip from a foothold into an abyss. This loss of footing is explicitly aligned with Milly's death: in an echo of her act of turning her face to the wall, Densher is "driven . . . to the wall" (379) by Lord Mark's disclosure of the engagement. Images of fall and of the abyss resonate through the final chapters; Densher's very favor with Aunt Maud "cut[s] . . . the ground from under their feet" (448), and he is pushed into an "abyss," defeated by the "false footing" of Milly's consideration for him (395, 245). He finally ends up in the oxymoronic dilemma of finding his standpoint or foothold in the abyss itself: "His main support really was his original idea, which didn't leave him, of waiting for the deepest depth his predicament could sink him to" (390). In a displacement of the Christological role thematically assigned to Milly, Densher undergoes the "crucifixion" of his obligation to "make up to her" (353). And the final chapters replay ironically the Bronzino episode, with its intimation of "facing" a deadly specular other: in chapter 30, he circles the café where Lord Mark sits, studying his face behind the glass

(365).[24] Both Mark's and Sir Luke Strett's faces present to Densher a radical blankness that proves not only unreadable, but potentially fatal: he "turn[s] cold at the image" of Strett's impassive face (392) as if struck dead or turned to stone.

Densher's suspicion that "I may be safely left to kill my own cause" (62) is thus ironically fulfilled, literally so by Milly's death and figuratively by his break with Kate. His error activates his punning surname: Densher turns out to be decisively denser than Milly who, to recall Lord Mark's comment about the Bronzino, goes them, all round, one better. (The text itself plays on this pun: "Kate turned her head away as if really at last almost tired of his density," 341.) As the narrator observes, "they had succeeded too well" (448). On the one hand, Densher's courtship of Milly metaleptically conjures up an intimacy after the fact, creating the affect it was meant to simulate. As he says of Kate's rejection of Lord Mark, his lie becomes "a phenomenon requiring a reason" (384) in a metaleptic reversal of cause and effect.[25] On the other, it retrospectively cancels out his love for Kate; as she notes in a formulation whose past perfect tense alludes to this causal trick or distortion, "you won't have loved *me*" (410)—the text emphasizes this reading by leaving unsaid the implied repetition of "for nothing" from her earlier statement ("[s]he won't have loved you for nothing"). Infidelity appears not merely an intersubjective theme, but a linguistic operation beyond Kate's, Densher's, or James's control. If, as the narrator says, "waiting was the game of dupes" (200), Kate and Densher unwittingly become the dupes of their own game, whose double-edged or double-dealing quality enables it to "return" upon them (399). Densher's lie similarly returns upon itself, due to a curious performative effect that actualizes the intention it would simulate. It turns, tropes, or gives the lie to his love for Kate.

24. For a psychosexual argument that reads the novel's thematics of the gaze in terms of a male homoeroticism in this and other late scenes, see Michael Moon, "Sexuality and Visual Terrorism in *The Wings of the Dove*," *Criticism*, XXVIII (1986), 427–43.

25. "[N]othing perhaps was just so sharp as the odd influence of their present conditions on their view of their past ones. It was as if they hadn't known how 'thick' they had originally become, as if, in a manner, they had really fallen to remembering more passages of intimacy than there had in fact at the time quite been room for" (247).

A similar dilemma is the burden of an extraordinary passage in James's preface, which asserts that a work of art is founded on a necessary blindness to its own way of being. The work of art, the passage says, is like a bridge whose piers or supports are known to be illusory; yet the bridge stands despite the acknowledgment of this illusion. James writes: "the bridge spans the stream, after the fact, in apparently complete independence of these properties, the principal grace of the original design. *They* were an illusion, for their necessary hour; but the span itself, whether of a single arch or many, seems by the oddest chance in the world to be a reality" (*AN*, 297). The artist seems to enjoy the mastery of his finished work, but that work is itself only a substitute or copy of its original conception, of which he is already the unwitting dupe. This interdependence of mastery and illusion may account for the affectively charged language of the preface, which speaks of the novel as containing "secrets and compartments," "possible treacheries and traps" (*AN*, 289). The abysmal trap of its plot turns out to be one from which its "designer" (*AN*, 292) is not exempt. Adverting to the novel's motif of masks and faces, James himself appears to have experienced his text as a play of concealment and exposure: "the motive of 'The Wings of the Dove' . . . was to worry me at moments by a sealing-up of its face—though without prejudice to its again, of a sudden, fairly grimacing with expression" (*AN*, 309–10). His cryptic complaint about the "misplaced pivot" in Book Fifth (*AN*, 306) itself appears, in this light, misplaced. If it alludes to the Bronzino episode, then James's remark may reflect the causal and proleptic power of the Bronzino portrait itself, which appears similarly misplaced or even disproportionate. The misplaced pivot also describes the novel's representational strategy, which displaces and effaces its designated center of consciousness. Yet this displacement only illustrates the universal decentering of the central consciousness—what James calls "the inveterate displacement of [the] general centre" (*AN*, 302). As in *Roderick Hudson,* the gaps and lapses that James identifies are causal as well as formal. The displacement of the center is inveterate, not contingent; universal, not local.

This may be the burden of the numismatic metaphor that figures the disproportion between the novel's "false and deformed" halves, or between what James terms the center and circumference of its representational scheme. The center and circumference correspond, respectively, to Milly's "case" and the cases of those affected by her. James notes: "could I but make my medal hang free, its obverse and its reverse, its face and its back, would beautifully become optional for the spectator. I somehow wanted them correspondingly embossed, wanted them inscribed and figured with an equal salience" (*AN*, 294). But the novel's latter half strikes James as disproportionate and foreshortened, remarkable "for foreshortening at any cost, for imparting to patches the value of presences" (*AN*, 302). Like Milly herself, the novel appears "past patching" (229).

This medal metaphor evokes the "bright hard medal" of *What Maisie Knew*, "one face of which is somebody's right and ease and the other somebody's pain and wrong" (*AN*, 143), and also recalls James's account of the solidity and mass of the narrative block assigned to Kate: "Terms of amplitude, terms of atmosphere, those terms, and those terms only, in which images assert their fulness and roundness, their power to revolve, so that they have sides and backs, parts in the shade as true as parts in the sun" (*AN*, 296). The power to revolve imputed to this implicit coin image suggests a chiastic reversibility like the causal turn we have seen inscribed in the novel as a whole. The two sides of James's medal in the *Wings* preface, the center and circumference of the novel's formal and causal structure, Milly's case and her effect on those around her—all of these are disproportionate or incommensurate, pointing to a congenital disproportion or incommensurability in the novel which James's preface both discovers and covers over.

The author's positing of the illusory bridge over the abyss therefore remains an error, but a necessary error. James concludes:

> some acute mind ought surely to have worked out by this time the "law" of the degree in which the artist's energy fairly depends on his fallibility. How much and how often, and in what connexions and with what almost infinite variety, must he be a dupe, that of his prime object, to be at all measurably a master, that of his actual substitute for it—or in other words at all appreciably to exist? (*AN*, 297)

The possibility that energy and fallibility, mastery and dupery, or truth and lie, are radically entwined or even two faces of the same coin, is the law—if this can still be called a law—of narrative, and of language, itself. The capacity of language to turn against itself is, like death, one law from which none of us is exempt. Even to recognize the mastery of the Master's formulation is to become the dupe of the abysmal trap it names. Like Densher, only on the face of it do we experience a mastery of that by which we have been duped all along.

6

The Golden Bowl and the Shattered Vessel
of Consciousness

Like *The Wings of the Dove*, *The Golden Bowl* adopts a deliberately divided
reflective center. According to James's preface, the novel presents the
"register" of the Prince's consciousness in the first volume and Maggie's,
whose "function . . . matches exactly with his" in the second.[1] Yet this
assertion of a formal match or symmetry between the novel's halves is
countered by James's elaboration of the differing representational authority of its centers of consciousness. The Prince controls only those
elements in which he is not "superceded" by Fanny Assingham, whereas
Maggie "duplicates, as it were, her value and becomes a compositional
resource . . . as well as a value intrinsic" (*AN*, 329, 330). "Register"
carries here a slight economic, as well as narrative, resonance; and we
may wonder how the doubling or duplication effect ascribed to Maggie
is to be reconciled with James's assertion of equity between the novel's
two registers. His scrutiny of the novel's representational "match" echoes
the various forms of matching that are in question in *The Golden Bowl*:
the punning place-name Matcham, Adam's warning that he is not the
"ideal match" for Charlotte, the equivocal "matchless beauty" of Charlotte's and the Prince's position after the marriages, and Charlotte's ability

---

1. On the decentering effects of the novel's bipartite structure, see Margery Sabin,
The Dialect of the Tribe (New York, 1987), 65–105; Joseph Boone, "Modernist Maneu-
verings in the Marriage Plot: Breaking Ideologies of Gender and Genre in James's *The
Golden Bowl*," *PMLA*, CI (1986), 374–88; and Lloyd Davis, *Sexuality and Textuality in
Henry James: Reading Through the Virginal* (New York, 1988).

to "match," "by perfect parity of imagination," Amerigo's sense of the adulterous opportunity offered at Matcham.[2]

James's insistence on the match or parity between the novel's formal halves is ironically qualified by the other kind of matching evoked in the preface. He recounts his discovery, in rereading his recent works on the occasion of the New York Edition, of a continuity of intention and vision between his past and present authorial selves. In James's remarkable figure for this equivalence, his own past vision, "superimposed on my own as an image in cut paper is applied to a sharp shadow on a wall, matches, at every point, without excess or deficiency." As J. Hillis Miller has pointed out, this odd image reverses the expected priority between shadow and superimposed image, giving temporal priority to James's present vision and so implying the "original" vision to be a retrospective construction made to "match" his present intention.[3] Further, the trope for rereading as the retracing of one's steps in the snow does double and contradictory duty, for it is made to figure first this ideal parity of intention and then the discrepancy of intention he discerns on rereading his early novels. On one hand, James writes that, in revisiting his recent works, he sinks comfortably into the "very footprints" of his original intention. On the other, this figure acquires the opposite meaning when applied to his rereading of the early novels, in which case his inability to repeat his "original tracks" without "break[ing] the surface in other places" signals the inevitability of such "deviations and differences, which became thus things not of choice, but of immediate and perfect necessity" (*AN*, 336). James's revision of his own figure revokes his initial claim to parity between past and present intention, since the deviation he finds is inevitable rather than fortuitous, constitutive rather than contingent.

The preface's concern with the match between past and present authorial consciousness both parallels and figures its concern with the match between the novel's formal halves, the Prince's and Maggie's successive registers as reflective centers. The New York Edition, with its labors of revision and of the critical metanarrative to which the prefaces aspire,

2. Henry James, *The Golden Bowl* (1904; rpr. Harmondsworth, U.K., 1966), 176, 221, 260.

3. Miller, *The Ethics of Reading,* 112.

itself attempts to impose both a synchronic stylistic unity and a continuity of authorial consciousness—not only on the individual texts selected for inclusion there, but on James's oeuvre as a whole. More than formal perfection is at stake in his reflections on *The Golden Bowl,* which takes as its titular germ the very figure of the vessel of consciousness. Its eponymous metaphor both concretizes and interrogates James's recurrent tropes of the cup, vessel, or receptacle of consciousness, and so mounts a critique of his characteristic representational strategy. Further, the "latent crack" (423) in the golden bowl figures the latent crack, the causal and formal fissure, in *The Golden Bowl* itself.

The bowl is inscribed in a rich figurative network of cups, vessels, and receptacles. In one of its aspects, this figurative system is self-reflexive and narratological in its implications. Holland observes that the shopkeeper, with his ceremonial presentation of "My Golden Bowl," and whose "heterogeneous" array of "old chased and jewelled artistry" (104, 99, 100) powerfully resonates with the "dusky, crowded, heterogeneous back-shop of the mind" ascribed to the writer ("a wary dealer in precious odds and ends") in the preface to *The Portrait of a Lady* (*AN,* 47), unmistakably figures the author.[4] James calls attention to the bowl's narrative status: "It told its story" (108), Amerigo says of his detection of its hidden crack, a remark fulfilled when the bowl "turn[s] witness" (410) after its purchase. Its character as a representational metaphor is further underlined by Amerigo and Charlotte's exchange in the shop, which turns on the problem of the bowl's referential status. Charlotte rejects Amerigo's offer of a gift on the grounds that it would have "no reference," would be a "*ricordo* of nothing," and Maggie and Fanny will later debate what the bowl "represents" (101, 412). The bowl's "conscious perversity" and "stupid elegance" align it with the lovers and especially with Charlotte, whose decisive rejection at the end of the novel is signaled when the

4. Holland, *The Expense of Vision,* 345–46, and David McWhirter, *Desire and Love in Henry James: A Study of the Late Novels* (Cambridge, U.K., 1989), 158–59. Davis contends that the bowl embodies the text's own "praxis of unreadability" (*Sexuality and Textuality in Henry James,* 182). On the self-reflexive implications of the bowl, see also Pearson, "The Novel to End All Novels: *The Golden Bowl*"; and Meili Steele, "The Drama of Reference in James's *The Golden Bowl,*" *Novel: A Forum on Fiction,* XXI (1987), 73–88.

Prince names her to Maggie as "stupid" (412, 411, 533). By describing the bowl as "simple," the narrator echoes ironically the Prince's equivocal resolution "simply to be, with [Charlotte], always simple—and with the very last simplicity"—a formulation whose repetition, qualification, and variation belie its claim to simplicity (104, 92). For Maggie, the bowl comes to figure the specious basis or foundation of both marriages ("It was *on* the whole thing that Amerigo married me," 415). Its "circular foot" (104) accordingly combines the image of a basis, ground, or standpoint with the circular causality of the "vicious circle" (292; *Notebooks*, 74), the conundrum by which the novel's center of consciousness unwittingly precipitates the adulterous narrative crossings she would preempt.

Charlotte and Amerigo's discussion of the bowl's possible value as a ricordo—a souvenir, record, memory, or warning—further points to a curious coercive power that attaches to the novel's eponymous metaphor. One way to describe its plot would be to say that the bowl is transfigured from a ricordo of nothing to a ricordo of the narrative we know as *The Golden Bowl*. A ricordo is temporally double-edged, both memorial and proleptic. The bowl is already a ricordo in the second sense, as the Prince recognizes when he says he would fear for his marriage in accepting the flawed bowl as a gift. Only later does it become a ricordo in the first sense. It is as if the bowl calls into being its own referent (significantly, Charlotte and Amerigo invoke it when planning the outing to Gloucester), effecting the causal slippage suggested in this passage: "The sense of the past revived for him nevertheless as it had not yet done: it made that other time somehow meet the future close, interlocking with it, before his watching eyes, as in a long embrace of arms and lips" (227). This image of an interlocking of past and future, of memory and prolepsis, is suggestive of the coercive power of figuration, for its sexualized simile is actualized by the embrace between Charlotte and Amerigo that concludes this scene. The bowl, which figures both the ground of narrative and its antithesis, both the decorative surface of James's standpoint and the abyss behind or beneath, signifies the doubly figuring and disfiguring capacity of metaphor itself. This is the capacity to posit or "put" ("we recognise betimes that to 'put' things is very exactly and responsibly and interminably to do them," *AN,* 347) which, like the bridge that spans the stream despite the illusory character of its piers in the *Wings of the Dove* preface (*AN,* 297), remains a "figured void," a catachrestic positing or veiling over an abyss or "bottomless gulf" (488, 293).

Like all those figures misleadingly termed controlling metaphors, the bowl resists both our own and the characters' attempts to fix and stabilize its meaning. Fanny Assingham equates the bowl with Maggie's suspicion about her husband and stepdaughter, insisting that "your whole idea has a crack" (420). But her literalism backfires when she shatters the "precious vessel" (421), much like Kate's destruction of Milly's letter. Rather than destroy Maggie's evidence, as Fanny intends, she activates and empowers it in a theatrical tour de force that fortuitously coincides with the Prince's entrance. The bowl's destruction actualizes Maggie's fear that her faith in the Prince may "go to smash" (37), as well as recalls the kiss by which the lovers seal their pledge: "everything broke up, broke down, gave way, melted and mingled. Their lips sought their lips, their pressure their response and their response their pressure" (237). This passage, whose chiastic syntax reflects the plot's adulterous crossing, anticipates the smashing of the bowl not only in the image of breaking but in its "violence" (237), which fulfills the shopkeeper's prediction of its fate if dashed "with violence—say upon a marble floor" (106). The bowl splits into three pieces, two halves and a "solid detached foot" (423), corresponding to the novel's own formal halves and the representational "footing" of the reflector method itself. Its splitting not only figures the novel's erotic triangulation, the most immediate referent of the three pieces Maggie gathers, but figuratively shatters the vessel of consciousness itself, actualizing James's characterization of the novel as a form that appears "more true to its character in proportion as it strains, or tends to burst, with a latent extravagance, its mould" (*AN,* 46).

The bowl's splitting into three pieces further reflects the novel's divided deployment of the central intelligence, whose narrative function is in effect dispersed (despite the preface's claim) among the Prince, Fanny, and Maggie.[5] Fanny is an antithetical or parodic reflector whose most

5. Maggie finds that "she could carry but two of the fragments at once." Of this detail, Alexander Welsh comments: "The piece left on the floor has to be Adam's. Latterly the entire object was to have been Adam's, a birthday gift for the man who already has collected most of the other things in the world for his museum in American City; but

egregious misreading is her triumphant conviction of Charlotte's and
Amerigo's "straightness," an oxymoronic "dim illumination" that coincides ironically with their Gloucester assignation (274, 277). (Sharon
Cameron points out that "Assingham" puns on the assignment or assignation of meaning.[6]) As Leo Bersani remarks, Fanny embodies an "interpretive promiscuity at work in art itself": "The extraordinary section
at the end of the first part in which Fanny figures out what will happen
in the second part is a kind of critique *in medias res* in which the dependence of novelistic plot on critical speculation is introduced as a literal
possibility within the novel itself."[7] Like Maisie, she further stands for
language's capacity for unforeseeable "appreciation" as against the re-
pressive and recuperative narrative control enforced by Maggie in Volume
II. Her antithetical "aggressive peace" (440) mirrors Maggie's passive-
aggressive narrative mode. Fanny adopts as formal principle the ideal of
symmetry that Maisie only unwittingly effects: she "fall[s] in love with
the beautiful symmetry of my plan" from a sense that the others "were
making a mess of such charming material . . . wasting it and letting it
go" (289). In the spirit of the Jamesian artist, Fanny advocates art's "sublime economy" against life's "splendid waste" (*AN*, 120), but cannot
prevent the ramification of her symmetrical interpersonal scheme beyond
its imposed formal economy. Her propensity for matching gets out of
control; like James's own in *What Maisie Knew*, her narrative line expands
into a "magic web" (227), and the "incalculable twists and turns" of her
interpretive constructions (277) figure the potential for deviation that
James imputes to representation itself in his preface to *The Ambassadors*.

Although the text worries over Fanny's potential for breakdown or
"collapse," it is the Prince who exemplifies the Jamesian reflector's "falsity
of position" (238, 252). Like Strether, he undergoes an extinction of sorts

---

the bowl will not be so collected. . . . A birthday celebration that was to have been and
a symbolic death of Adam Verver coincide with Maggie's initiation." See *Strong Representations: Narrative and Circumstantial Evidence in England* (Baltimore, 1992), 253.

6.   Cameron, *Thinking in Henry James,* 118. Ruth Bernard Yeazell rightly sees Fanny
as a "parody of the Jamesian artist"; see *Language and Knowledge in the Late Novels of Henry
James* (Chicago, 1971), 97.

7.   Bersani, *A Future for Astyanax,* 149. R. P. Blackmur observes that the Assinghams
"create the scandal they would excuse"; see *Studies in Henry James,* ed. Veronica A. Makowsky (New York, 1983), 141.

at the end of his titular volume, and the transition to Maggie's narrative replays the cluster of figures we have elsewhere seen associated with the collapse of the reflective center: the overflowing cup or receptacle, the "snapping" aligned in the critical prefaces with the broken lifeline of the center of consciousness (311), and the representational impasse of "a mere dead wall, a lapse of logic, a confirmed bewilderment" (266) equivalent to Hyacinth's "bewilderment," Maisie's "pretty pass," Roderick's "dead blank of my mind," or the "dead wall" of Isabel Archer's meditative vigil in *The Portrait of a Lady*[8] (as also in the "house of fiction" passage of James's preface).

Maggie is James's most equivocal transfiguration of the reflective center, an unseeing reflector whose figuratively "absent," "sightless," or "bandaged" eyes suggest a willed blindness or refusal of knowledge (154, 336, 423).[9] But like Rowland's, her "projected vision" (315) carries a coercive causal power. Her exertion of revisionary authorial control when she pursues Charlotte for the purpose of presenting her with the "right volume" (508), or the narrator's comparison of her to an author directing a rehearsal (458), are only the most explicit markers of this compositional power. It is figured especially by her capacity for "translation," as her interpretive activities in Volume Two are termed (326, 493, 521). Like the narrator of *What Maisie Knew*, Maggie in effect becomes a Jamesian narrator who translates Amerigo's and Charlotte's consciousness, treating them as receptive vessels for her own speculative projections and so constructing the "consciousness" she would seem only to mediate.

What the preface calls Maggie's value as "compositional resource" is,

---

8. James, *The Portrait of a Lady*, 461.

9. On the problematic of the gaze in the novel, see Griffin, *The Historical Eye*, 57–90; Porter, *Seeing and Being*, 152–64; Sabin, *The Dialect of the Tribe*, 82–105; Seltzer, *Henry James and the Art of Power*, 59–95; Jean-Christophe Agnew, "The Consuming Visions of Henry James," in *The Culture of Consumption: Critical Essays on American History 1880–1980*, ed. Richard Wightman Fox and T. Jackson Lears (New York, 1983), 65–100; Marcia Ian, "Consecrated Diplomacy and the Concretion of Self," *Henry James Review*, VII (1985), 27–33; and Cheryl B. Torsney, "Specula(riza)tion in *The Golden Bowl*," *Henry James Review*, XII (1991), 141–46. Marianna Torgovnick writes suggestively of James's allusions in the closing passage to Aristotle and *Oedipus Rex*, allusions that invoke the play on "seeing" and "knowing" as well as the themes of incest and blindness; see her *Closure in the Novel* (Princeton, 1981), 151.

I suspect, this power of translation. The capacity for duplication James attributes to Maggie is precisely this self-doubling as reflector and narrator, a duplication that doubles her narrative value and so "raise[s] her higher" (485). In one sense, then, Maggie occupies the "false position" (303) of the Jamesian reflector. She thinks herself a "scapegoat" (457) and, in keeping with the narrative economy of the center of consciousness, incurs a debt that mounts "like a column of figures" (354). But thanks to the logic of translation or rhetorical substitution intrinsic to the reflector, this indebtedness—what the narrator calls "the refuse of her innocent economy" (328)—is itself transferred and displaced to the Prince and Charlotte, the surrogate reflectors who pay vicariously for Maggie's "arrears" (200). Charlotte, not Maggie, is relegated to a gilded cage (454), to the "chasm" or abyss of her separation from Amerigo (in a reminiscence of *Wings,* Maggie says of her that "I feel somehow as if she were dying," 521, 532); and Amerigo similarly finds himself "straitened and tied" (430) in the figurative "prison" or "locked cage" of the encaged central consciousness (526).

The critical archive on *The Golden Bowl* notoriously divides over whether Maggie's authorial power is destructive or beatific, whether her successful recovery and repair of the two marriages is ironic or redemptive in its implications. The text not only allows but demands both readings, and it is here that the novel's affiliation to *What Maisie Knew* is clearest. *The Golden Bowl*'s muted yet ambivalent treatment of what Maggie calls her own and Adam's lack of "natural relations" (40) elaborates the latent incestuous element of the conclusion of *What Maisie Knew,* which stops short of introducing the adolescent Maisie into the plot's erotic tangle.[10] Like Maisie, Maggie inadvertently engineers the plot's chiastic erotic entanglement, bringing together first her father and Charlotte—her mediation extending even to Adam's equivocal assurance to Charlotte that

10. Holland comments on the "curiously short-circuited relations which prevail among the four" in *The Golden Bowl* (*The Expense of Vision,* 337). On the question of incest, see Linda Zwinger, *Daughters, Fathers, and the Novel: The Sentimental Romance of Heterosexuality* (Madison, Wis., 1991), 76–95. In "Sexuality and the Aesthetic in *The Golden Bowl,*" *Henry James Review,* XIV (1993), 55–71, Hugh Stevens investigates erotic, and especially masochistic, fantasy in the novel.

Maggie will speak "for" him (180)[11]—and then the adulterous lovers. Like Maisie and Milly—the three names all but rhyme—Maggie illustrates a "split between conviction and action" that coincides with her "knowing everything" (426) and which, like the split in the golden bowl, portends a split or fissure between knowledge and action that disables any ethical judgment about the redemptive or destructive consequences of her actions. Maggie's oxymoronic "unfortunate virtue" antithetically "undo[es]" the "decency" of others (97), making right into wrong (142) and producing a chiastic intermingling of innocence and guilt, like the two-faced coin of the preface to *Maisie*. The germ of *The Golden Bowl* is similarly "adulterine" (*Notebooks,* 115) in the multiple senses of adulterous, spurious, counterfeit, or adulterated.

As in *Maisie*, too, the disequilibrium resulting from this adulterine germ engenders the causal paradox of the "vicious circle" (292). Despite Fanny's speculative and Maggie's revisionary efforts, no amount of narrative elaboration can correct, set right, or otherwise account for its circular causal logic. Thanks to its "rotary motion" and "inevitable rotary way" (*Notebooks,* 75, 74), Maggie's virtue undoes the decency it would promote, the lovers' "good faith" itself produces their "false position" (281), and the remedy to the "funny form" of the marriages is indistinguishable from the "bottomless gulf" or abyss (316, 293) of the vicious circle itself. As Fanny inquires, "How in the world, with so much of a remedy, comes there to remain so much of what was to be obviated?" (203). The abysmal logic of the vicious circle is such that the remedy is identical to the error it would correct, much as the "steel hoop" (396) of Maggie's recovered intimacy with the Prince equivocally recalls the vicious circle it would remedy.

In *The Art of the Novel,* James proposes that the highest enjoyment of a work of art occurs "when we feel the surface, like the thick ice of the skater's pond, bear without cracking the strongest pressure we throw on it. The sound of the crack one may recognise, but never surely to call it a luxury" (*AN,* 304–305). Here, as in his characterization of the novel

---

11. See Bradbury's fine discussion of the ambiguous cumulative implications of "for," which play on the novel's themes of motivation and substitution (*Henry James: The Later Novels,* 143–44).

by its capacity to "burst with a latent extravagance" its mold (*AN*, 45–46), James suggests that the success of his art is to be measured by its willful testing or exertion of pressure upon its own narrative resources. *The Golden Bowl* allegorizes this exertion of pressure by extending the key Jamesian metaphors of the frangible mold and impenetrable surface into a notoriously dense and complex narrative. Maggie's interpretive activity is similarly figured in images of surface and depth. She studies the "impenetrable and inscrutable" facade of the imaginary pagoda, but finally eschews the strategy of the Jamesian penetrating imagination and adopts the principle of preserving an impenetrable surface of her own that "suffered no symptom anywhere to peep out" (301, 441). She not only represses the cause or ground of her action, the "thing hideously *behind*" (459), but herself becomes unreadable and impenetrable, a "blank, blurred surface" (466). The representational blank or eclipse typical of James's reflector fictions, the final renunciation of going behind that marks the critical ethical moments in the novels read here (Hyacinth's ethical crisis, Maisie's knowledge, the turn Milly would have given her act) becomes in *The Golden Bowl* the adopted strategy of the center of consciousness herself. By her refusal to posit any cause beneath the forms she preserves, Maggie deliberately obscures or disjoins the relation between cause and effect, "shuffl[ing] away every link between consequence and cause" (531).

But while she restores successfully the fragments of the marriages, Maggie's triumph is predicated upon a fiction as fragile as the narrative vessel of the reflector, the representational ground or standpoint that James's fictions both posit and dismantle. As others have commented, Maggie's authorial success is equivocal not least because it reinstates the Gilbert Osmond–like aestheticism which the novel would critique, the objectification implied by the Ververs' initial purchase of Charlotte and the Prince.[12] In a reminiscence of the crystal bowl, the novel's final scene "crystallize[s]" (540), the Prince and Charlotte assimilated to the object-world of Adam's collection as "human furniture" (541). This crystal-

12.   Freedman writes, "The nexus between aestheticization and will to power and the simultaneous valorizing of aesthetic forms and social conventions that James had satirized with such fervor in the figure of Osmond now enter his work as principles of affirmative value, as indeed the only value James can imagine" (*Professions of Taste*, 241.)

lization is attributed to Maggie's "inner vision" as reflector, which "fixe[s]" its objects into formal "attitude[s]" (343). Like Maisie, who cannot be worked into her novel's figurative economy and must be sacrificed in the interest of a final equilibrium, the "incomparable" Charlotte (543) provides the "basis" for closure, the ground "firm under their feet" (544). "*Le compte y est*" (541), Adam's comment as he and Maggie survey their collection, is such a gesture of closure: the double register of the idiom, which means both "they're all there" and "the account is correct," marks a closing of narrative accounts. Charlotte not only underwrites this triumphant accountability ("They were parting . . . absolutely on Charlotte's *value*," 545), but plays Hawthorne/Roderick to Maggie's James by "point[ing]" the "moral" of Maggie's authorial success (547).

But what moral is that? However successful her recovery of the shattered bowl and its referent in the marriages, Maggie is left, not in the false position of the reflector as displaced onto Charlotte, but in the false position of the Jamesian artist himself, who knows his beautiful bridge over the abyss to be supported by illusory piers. The text points to this negative knowledge when the narrator rather enigmatically terms Maggie's understanding of the adulterous lovers' relation a "figured void" and a "veiled" picture, "behind which she felt, indistinguishable, the procession of forms that had lost, all so pitifully, their precious confidence" (488–89). The referent of "their" is ambiguous: whose confidence in such forms has been lost? Have the forms themselves lost confidence in their ability to perpetuate illusion, or is it Charlotte and Amerigo who have lost confidence in the power of social forms to veil their secret relation? Further, Maggie's identification of these "forms" in the same sentence that pronounces them "indistinguishable" (and thus not forms at all, arguably) implies that her naming of them *as* forms is a potentially false and totalizing imposition. In any case, the passage suggests that the forms in question veil or cover over the void that lies beneath figure itself. We are reminded that James's preface to *The Golden Bowl* figures the reflective center as a veiling, "a convenient substitute or apologist for the creative power otherwise so veiled and disembodied" (*AN*, 327). The veil of figuration calls attention to the void or abyss it would cover.

Like the bowl, the "frail vessel" of the Jamesian reflector (as James quotes George Eliot, *AN,* 49) breaks "on lines and by laws of its own" (107). The "obscured figure" (445) of James's golden bowl is indeed a figure, not only for the vessel of consciousness, but for figuration itself, as the preface makes clear by underlining the tropological character of the shop where the bowl is acquired: "the small shop was but a shop of the mind, of the author's projected world, in which objects are primarily related to each other" (*AN,* 334). However obscure or ungrounded, like the recurring tropes of card games which are uncannily actualized by the bridge game, and which oscillate uneasily between literal and figurative, such figures are the catachrestic positings that separate us from the abyss. The moral Maggie points on the last page is perhaps this negative insight into the ungrounded status of such forms. Although it is often read as affirming the redemptive power of form, *The Golden Bowl* reveals that such redemption, however efficacious, is built over a void or abyss. James's last completed novel in this sense reveals his master trope of the house of fiction to be an unstable "house of cards" (354)—albeit a house of cards that uncannily persists in standing.[13]

13.   Cf. the narrator of *The Sacred Fount,* whose "collapse" coincides with his discovery that his "palace of thought" is revealed to be a "house of cards" or "mere heap of disfigured fragments" (*The Sacred Fount* [1901; New York, 1953], 297, 262, 311).

7

Representational Awkwardness
in *The Awkward Age*

In *What Maisie Knew,* James has recourse to the so-called scenic method as an antidote to the expansive and unpredictable narrative ramifications of the "ironic center." The scenic method is indeed usually understood as antithetical to the center of consciousness, both in James's own and subsequent criticism. Associated especially with his novels of the 1890s, such as *The Awkward Age, The Other House,* and *The Tragic Muse,* the compositional system of the scenic method is thought to reflect James's preoccupation with the drama and, after his renunciation of writing for the stage, his desire to create a fictional correlative for dramatic form. The representational values attaching to the scenic method, which favors scene over exposition, mimesis over diegesis, the "scientific" (*AN,* 117) objectivity and economy of dialogue over the subjectivity and indirection of indirect discourse, appear the obverse of the central consciousness.

I propose to test this set of oppositions against *The Awkward Age* (1899), an exemplary scenic novel that is not only closely contemporary with *What Maisie Knew* (1897), but its thematic twin—the novels are often treated critically as a pair. *The Awkward Age* not only extends James's study of compromised innocence from Maisie's childhood and young adolescence to Nanda's late adolescence and young adulthood, but offers a representational sequel to *Maisie*'s allegory of the epistemology of the reflective center. *The Awkward Age* adopts as its compositional law the scenic strategy deployed in the final chapters of *What Maisie Knew,* taking as its narrative and conceptual germ the representational "awkwardness" (*Notebooks*, 166) that terminates *Maisie*.

Like *Maisie*, too, *The Awkward Age* reveals a continuity or complicity between thematic content and compositional method. Much as Maisie's adulteration is both the novel's subject and its representational requirement, so Nanda's "exposure" furnishes both the thematic germ and the narrative technique of *The Awkward Age*. In that Nanda's innocence is compromised precisely by the conversational freedom of her mother's circle, the scenic method of "dialogue organic and dramatic, speaking for itself, representing and embodying substance and form" (*AN*, 106) not only represents but enacts the exposure of Nanda's stigmatized knowledge.[1] Further, Nanda's fate replicates the "death of Maisie's childhood." Like Maisie's erasure as the residuum of the novel's compositional economy, Nanda's expulsion removes her not only from her mother's social circle but from the "vicious circle" of representation itself. Like the strategy of translation in *What Maisie Knew*, the compositional law of *The Awkward Age* causally intervenes by expelling from the novel's conversational and representational circle the character who embodies its thematic center. As the preface remarks, "The charm [of free talk] might be figured as dear to members of the circle consciously contributing to it, but it was none the less true that some sacrifice in some quarter would have to be made" (*AN*, 102). However much James may see the scenic method as the antidote to the narrative and causal aberrations that accompany his ironic centers, the rhetorical logic of the two compositional laws ultimately converges.

Like the center of consciousness, the scenic method is grounded in an aesthetics of sacrifice and renunciation. While the central consciousness entails a self-imposed limitation or restriction of perspective, the scenic method is grounded in a deliberate renunciation of "going behind":

> I myself have scarcely to plead the cause of "going behind," which is right and beautiful and fruitful in its place and order; but as the confusion of

---

1. Sergio Perosa comments that James's "experiment with the *roman dialogué* seems to be well suited to the story precisely because it is through the dialogues of the grown-ups that Nanda Brookenham is exposed to the danger of corruption" (*Henry James and the Experimental Novel* [Charlottesville, 1978], 69–70).

kinds is the inelegance of letters and the stultification of values, so to renounce that line utterly and do something quite different instead may become in another connexion the true course and the vehicle of effect. Something in the very nature, in the fine rigour, of this special sacrifice . . . lends it moreover a coercive charm; a charm that grows in proportion as the appeal to it tests and stretches and strains it, puts it powerfully to the touch. (*AN,* 111)

The scenic method thus supplants one formal sacrifice with another. Whereas the rhetorical logic of the reflector counters its own formal and epistemological claims, the scenic method abandons the discursive representation of consciousness for the avowed perspectivism of "the planned rotation of aspects." The passage strongly echoes James's assertion that the novel is "more true to its character in proportion as it strains, or tends to burst, with a latent extravagance, its mould." Much as the novel's integrity depends on its propensity for trying its own formal and epistemological structure, so the charm of the scenic law is proportionate to its testing and straining of its own limits. The preface to *The Wings of the Dove* explicitly proclaims the aesthetic benefits of the deliberate testing of the distinction between scene and picture: "Beautiful exceedingly . . . those occasions or parts of an occasion when the boundary line between picture and scene bears a little the weight of the double pressure" (*AN,* 182, 46, 300).

This is not to say that the center of consciousness and the scenic method are interchangeable or indistinguishable. James's representational categories are avowedly provisional and pragmatic, and it is axiomatic that fiction is always a hybrid of picture and scene.[2] Despite the traditional distinction in Anglo-American narratology between "showing" and "telling," scene is itself a phenomenological and figurative construction. And although the scenic method would claim to dispense altogether with indirect discourse—James states in the preface that "my first care *had* to be the covering of my tracks—lest I truly should be caught in the act of

---

2.   On the dual mimetic and diegetic character of the "scene" in fiction, see Gelley, *Narrative Crossings,* 155–71. Goetz usefully breaks down the traditional binary oppositions between the reflector and dramatic methods (*Henry James and the Darkest Abyss of Romance,* 13–14).

arranging, of organising dialogue to 'speak for itself' " (*AN,* 108)—a
fragmentary and abstracted central consciousness appears in *The Awkward
Age* in the repeatedly invoked "spectator" or "observer." One effect of
the novel's apparent renunciation of diegetic exposition or "going behind" is to render this vestigial narrator's own interpretive *locus standi* as
unstable as that of the Jamesian reflector. Todorov remarks that the effaced
narrator of *The Awkward Age* "does not, however, become a unifying
center; the narrator *sees* but he does not *know.*" In Todorov's view, this
indeterminacy and the oblique, self-reflexive qualities of the dialogue
render uncertain the ontological status of the events in question in the
novel.[3]

Despite the fluidity of the narrative categories that distinguish it from
the central consciousness, James's theorization of the scenic method rests
on an identifiable representational, even metaphysical, hierarchy. As Alexander Gelley usefully reminds us, the post-Jamesian tradition elaborated most fully by Percy Lubbock privileges scene as "the preeminent
representational mode of narrative art: it governs the internal organization of the narrative segments (selection of key incidents, dramatic con-
centration of the action) and is most powerfully and directly oriented
toward the act of reception. In this tradition the scene denotes the highest
degree of mimetic representation; it is designed to bring the reader into
the most unobstructed proximity to the subject matter of the narrative."[4]
Much is at stake in this valorization: its ideal of direct, unmediated com-
munication privileges immediacy over representation, perception over
language. In a sense, its culmination would be the achievement of an
(impossible) transparent language, or even the effacement of narrative *per
se.* Of course, these are Lubbock's prescriptive values and not James's. Yet
while James acknowledges the necessary inherence of diegesis in even
the most rigorously scenic text, his conceptualization of scene emphasizes
its visual and ostensive character. At the same time, the visual and pictorial
values by which he conceives the scenic method, for example in the
preface to *The Awkward Age,* are outlined in densely metaphorical lan-

3.   Tzvetan Todorov, "The Verbal Age," *Critical Inquiry,* IV (1977), 351–71, 366.
4.   Gelley, *Narrative Crossings,* 157.

guage whose rhetorical complexity undercuts the perceptual and spatial models they would uphold.

The preface opens with a gesture of preterition that at once deflects and attracts attention to the question of origins: James claims to recall, but desists from naming, the originary germ or "idea" of *The Awkward Age,* choosing rather to "leave my small secret undivulged" (*AN,* 98). The novel's germ remains "embalmed" (*AN,* 114), preserved for James's retrospective authorial appreciation yet concealed from the reader, much as Maisie "embalm[s] in her wonder" her own objects of consciousness (*AN,* 146). The organic maturation of the narrative germ is curiously collapsed into a salvific embalming, in a metaleptic enfolding of germination and negation that is echoed in the account of Nanda's awkward "irruption" into her mother's conversational circle. We may well associate this awkwardness with the text's unidentified and mystified germ. The novel concerns the social initiation of young women, the "mild revolution[ ]" induced by "the 'sitting downstairs,' from a given date, of the merciless maiden previously perched aloft." Like Maisie's "moral revolution," Hyacinth's "lively inward revolution," and Strether's "revolution," Nanda's fate is figured as a revolution or etymological turn. This "inevitable irruption of the ingenuous mind" is doubly compromising, for it threatens both freedom of conversation and the socially requisite innocence of the girl herself. Her exposure to licentious talk renders her unfit for marriage because, like an overfilled Jamesian vessel of consciousness, she knows too much. But as the preface also contends, her irruption into society is itself the condition of marriage. Hence the metaleptic bind James diagnoses: "A girl might be married off the day after her irruption, or better still the day before it, to remove her from the sphere of the play of mind" (*AN,* 100, 102, 103). The irruption in question marks a simultaneous preparation for and disqualification from marriage. As in *What Maisie Knew,* there is no middle ground between excessive innocence and excessive knowledge, the extremes played out diachronically in Aggie, only a radical slippage from infantile (*infans*) speechlessness to unspeakable knowledge. To have irrupted into society is to be always already unmarriageable. Aggie embodies the dubious ideal of being married off the day before her irruption, but even her marriage fails to prevent the ultimate slippage from knowledge of "nothing—but absolutely, utterly: not the least little tittle of anything," to the case of the "modern girl" who "knows too much."[5]

Nanda disrupts the binary logic of the irruption: she is "innocent and helpless" yet also "dreadfully damaged and depraved" (81), "so fearfully out of it, and yet . . . so fearfully in it" (150)—an outsider to, yet epistemologically complicit in, the sexual machinations of her mother's circle. "Coming down" to her mother's parlor from the nursery brings down her value on the marriage market ("Between you all, at any rate . . . you've brought me down," 166). On the other hand, her value is said to be "doubled" by Longdon's patronage. But like Maisie's "squaring," this doubling is achieved at the cost of removing her altogether from the "vicious circle"—as Mitchy terms Van's perverse sexual economy (108)—of exchange and representation alike. Nanda suffers a "retarded . . . incorporation" (AN, 105) which, like Maisie's oxymoronic "retarded knowledge" (66), repeats the metaleptic bind of the always already too late irruption. In keeping with the awkward logic of irruption, her social incorporation is simultaneously retarded and premature.[6] If the period before Nanda's descent from the nursery is "an age without a name" (165), her irruption marks a slippage from speechlessness to the unspeakable.

The awkwardness in question in the novel's title is therefore not only social (the transition from childhood to adulthood) and historical (the transition from the nineteenth to the twentieth century), but represen-

---

5. Henry James, *The Awkward Age* (1899; New York, 1981), 259, 230.

6. Silverman notes, "A surprising number of Jamesian characters are—like the infantile voyeur [in the Freudian primal scene]—conspicuously either too early or too late with respect to sexuality ("Too Early/Too Late: Subjectivity and the Primal Scene in Henry James," 162). For an illuminating study of the novel's feminization and critique of contemporary social scientific debates about class, cultural transmission, and reproduction, see Susan L. Mizruchi, "Reproducing Women in *The Awkward Age*," *Representations*, XXXVIII (1992), 101–30. In *The Daughter's Dilemma: Family Process and the Nineteenth-Century Domestic Novel* (Ann Arbor, 1991), 151–77, Paula Marantz Cohen reads *The Awkward Age* as culminating and revising a novelistic tradition, inaugurated by *Clarissa*, in which the "regulating daughter" embodies the symptomology of her pathogenic family system, and whose symptoms "function as homeostatic mechanisms, helping to maintain a precarious equilibrium within families that have been made subject to serious loss or disruption" (27).

tational. Although the scenic method would seem to exempt *The Awk-ward Age* from the narrative aberrations and deviations associated with the reflective center, James concedes that the novel illustrates the same discrepancy or incommensurability between mass and germ as do his center of consciousness fictions. He indeed classes it among the "comparative monsters" of his corpus, the works whose "unforeseen principle of growth" reveals "the quite incalculable tendency of a mere grain of subject-matter to expand and develop and cover the ground when conditions happen to favour it" (*AN,* 98). Like Nanda herself, who in her final interview with Longdon admits to "cover[ing] everything else with my own impossibility" (380), the novel's mystified germ exhibits a capacity for unexpected amplification, a susceptibility to the "false measurements" and "misplaced middles" of the Jamesian reflector. "Monstrous" and its variants are key words in *The Awkward Age,* applied especially to the ambient licentiousness of Mrs. Brook's circle. As in *The Art of the Novel,* monstrosity is what marks the unpredictable, perverse, or aberrant elements of language and narrative that produce the deflexions and deviations traced so insistently in the critical prefaces. It is thus opposed to the organic imagery of the germ. In one of its aspects, *The Awkward Age* revisits the prefaces' organicist theory of the novel as a natural object, playing ironically on their recurring images of germs, seeds, fruit, and so on. James aligns this organic figuration with the scenic method, whose "organic" dialogue aspires to the ideal narrative fruition from germ to perfected form.

What makes *The Awkward Age* a comparative monster, despite the preventative economy of scene? James remarks that the scenic method shares the theater's problem of pandering to public taste, which consumes uncritically the popular theater of the day "on the scale and with the smack of lips that mark the consumption of bread-and-jam by a children's school-feast" (*AN,* 106). His figure resonates oddly with the novel's own schoolroom thematics, which also appears obliquely in his explanation of the ensuing aesthetic bind for the artist:

Make the thing you have to convey, make the picture you have to paint, at all rich and complex, and you cease to be clear. Remain clear—and with the clearness required by the infantine intelligence of any public consenting to see a play—and what becomes of the "importance" of your subject? If it's important by any other critical measure than the little foot-rule the "produced" piece has to conform to, it is predestined to be a muddle. (*AN,* 112)

James's representational dilemma corresponds neatly to the novel's thematic conflict: like Mrs. Brook, he is faced with the necessity to accommodate an infantine audience by simplifying his dialogue to their level of understanding—dumbing it down, as it were.[7] To make such an accommodation is "to renounce the finer thing for the coarser," a concession James imputes to Ibsen and Dumas (*AN,* 112). This simplification would be the obverse of the narrator's translation of Maisie's point of view into figures not yet at her command, and the novel dramatizes its consequences in Longdon and Edward Brookenham, naive readers who require remedial translation of the talk around them (whereas Longdon's incomprehension is generational and social, Edward's is congenital). Both are comically inept with figurative language, especially with the racy and slangy currency of the Brook circle.[8] Like *What Maisie Knew, The Awkward Age* thus turns on a problem of naming or translation, and the trope of translation appears in the preface in connection with James's spectatorship of the English social awkwardness portrayed in the novel: "In circles highly civilised the great things, the real things . . . have ever, for the outsider's, for the critic's use, to be translated into terms—terms in the distinguished name of which . . . more than one situation of the type I glance at had struck me as all irresistibly appealing" (*AN,* 103).

Yet although its compositional tenet is antithetical to that of *What*

7. For an analysis of the correspondence between the novel's plot and the representational problematic outlined in James's preface, see Stuart Culver, "Censorship and Intimacy: Awkwardness in *The Awkward Age*," *English Literary History,* XLVIII (1981), 368–86. Culver traces a conflict between a Continental theory of literality aligned with the Duchess, according to which word and meaning coincide, and an English theory of linguistic obliquity "where meaning is always something other than its verbal formalization" (375).

8. As Bradbury observes, Longdon is figuratively opposed to "the prevailing verbal inflation and moral disintegration" (he "maintained the full value of the word," 39), though his attempt to bribe Van coincides with his increasing (and damning) conversational ease in the novel's debased verbal currency of slang and euphemism (*Henry James: The Later Novels,* 26).

Maisie Knew, The Awkward Age perversely repeats that novel's unwitting adulteration of Maisie by the narrator's figures. Like Mrs. Brook, James refuses to compromise the quality of his "talk," with the consequence that Nanda is exposed despite and because of her capacity to "expose everything and criticize" (252). Unrestrained talk is the novel's performative representational system as well as its theme—a homology underlined by James's account of the novel's composition. He recalls that

> in sketching my project for the conductors of the periodical I have named I drew on a sheet of paper—and possibly with an effect of the cabalistic, it now comes over me, that even anxious amplification may have but vainly attenuated—the neat figure of a circle consisting of a number of small rounds disposed at equal distance about a central object. The central object was my situation, my subject in itself, to which the thing would owe its title, and the small rounds represented so many distinct lamps. . . . Each of my "lamps" would be the light of a single "social occasion" in the history and intercourse of the characters concerned, and would bring out to the full the latent colour of the scene in question and cause it to illustrate, to the last drop, its bearing on my theme. I revelled in this notion of the Occasion as a thing by itself, really and completely a scenic thing, and could scarce name it, while crouching amid the thick arcana of my plan, with a large enough O. (*AN*, 109–10)

This resembles the narrative plan of *Wings,* with a central subject illuminated by surrounding reflectors and the whole unified by Milly's consciousness (*AN*, 300). Here, though James identifies a central structure that underwrites *The Awkward Age,* his figuration leaves indeterminate the status of this center. Although the novel's center is described as having a "latent colour" which the surrounding lamps merely illuminate, the lamp metaphor leaves open the possibility that this color is projected by the lamps and not an intrinsic property of the center itself. And the novel's structural principle is ultimately identical neither with the surrounding reflectors nor with the central figure itself, for the scenic achievement of the "Occasion" is produced by the interplay between obscure center and illuminating periphery. Rather than locate a narrative center or origin, James's schema describes a decentering or centrifugal diffusion.

Further, this complex figure of concentric circles or "rounds" around a central object—a figure also repeated by the "O" of "Occasion"—resonates with both Mrs. Brook's circle and the "vicious circle" (108) or "going round" of sexual intrigue, associated especially with Van's "sacred terror" (227). (This "O" is also repeated in Edward Brookenham's characteristic "Oh!," the Jamesian place-holder for the unspeakable.) How to distinguish the rotary logic of the center of consciousness from the "planned rotation of aspects," as James refers to the scenic method (*AN*, 182)? If Sergio Perosa is correct in identifying the "central object" of James's figure with Nanda herself,[9] there appears a complicitous homology between the plot's round of sexual intrigue and the narrative round of which Nanda is center, between the circle of licentious talk and the circle of representation. Elsewhere, James famously figures the imposition of narrative closure as the drawing of a circle: "Really, universally, relations stop nowhere, and the exquisite problem of the artist is eternally but to draw, by a geometry of his own, the circle within which they shall happily *appear* to do so" (*AN*, 5). To enter Mrs. Brook's circle is to enter the vicious circle, as in *What Maisie Knew* and *The Golden Bowl*, of representation itself.

In one important respect, however, James's novel departs from his theoretical prescriptions in the preface. Whereas the preface asserts that the "intellectually helpless compromise" (*AN*, 103) of accommodating the infantine public results in the "muddle" of popular drama, Mrs. Brook's opposite tactic of preserving good talk at all costs produces precisely "a muddle, a compromise, a monstrosity" (61). *The Awkward Age* simultaneously fulfills and ruptures the perfect fusion of substance and form James claims for it—the fusion which the preface equivocally terms a "break down" (*AN*, 115). On the one hand, Cashmore's crime of "mixing [Nanda] up" with "his not very tidy muddles" (141) is surreptitiously duplicated by the novel's representational strategy, which exposes Nanda to the conversational licence Maisie is spared. On the other, the novel reveals a fissure between substance and form that qualifies the preface's theoretical formulation. For the concession of re-

9. "Nanda, more than a center of consciousness like Maisie (and, significantly, she has no need for *ficelles*), became a *structural* center and pivot of the dramatic construction—a construction which for James himself, who sketched it in the Preface of the novel, took the form of concentric rings" (Perosa, *Henry James and the Experimental Novel*, 70).

nouncing "the finer thing for the coarser" that James claims to avoid by ignoring the commercial imperatives of the infantine public intelligence is reintroduced by the novel's central event: Van's renunciation of the finer Nanda in favor of the coarser (but unobjectionably infantine) Aggie, the hypocritical and opportune renunciation on which the entire story turns. The novel's thematic enactment of the compromise it avoids at the level of representational strategy may explain James's characterization of *The Awkward Age* as "monstrous."

Figured as a "small sprig of tender green" (116) "plant[ed]" in her mother's drawing room (64), Nanda is identified with the germ, seed, or slip of the novel itself, said to have been "sprouted in that vast nursery of sharp appeals . . . London" (*AN*, 99). "Irruption," James's term in the preface for Nanda's introduction to her mother's circle, plays on this imagery of germination. But it also suggests a rupture, breaking, or bursting like the "cracking and bursting" James attributes to the "mould" of the drama (*AN*, 115). Irruption therefore designates both the organic fruition James claims for the scenic method and the disruption of this organicist teleology. The scenic method, no less than the reflective center, turns out to be vulnerable to the "inevitable deviation" the preface to *The Ambassadors* imputes to representation itself. The circulation of figure can no more be controlled or circumscribed by the "roundabout and devious" scenic principle (*Notebooks*, 115) than by the reflective center.

The scenic method's deviation from an organicist theory of representation is the burden of what the preface terms "deflexion." Whereas the novel is "the perfect paradise of the loose end," drama is ideally economical, "with the loose end as gross an impertinence on its surface, and as grave a dishonour, as the dangle of a snippet of silk or wool on the right side of a tapestry" (*AN*, 114). As an exemplary scenic novel, *The Awkward Age* is constructed "on absolutely scenic lines" and "abides without a moment's deflexion by the principle of the stage-play" (*AN*, 115). Yet James retrospectively detects a "deflexion from simplicity" (*AN*, 114) in the novel's considerable complication of the scenic ideal exemplified by "Gyp" (Martel de Janville, the author of numerous dialogue novels). The multiple meanings of deflection are suggestive here in light of the figuration of the preface: a turning or bending from a

straight line, change of direction, deviation from course, bending of a
ray of light from a straight line in optics, a turning or conversion of a
thing to something different from its natural use, a turn, bend, or curve;
a turning of word or phrase from its form, application, or grammatical
use (*OED* 3). This last archaic sense, which strongly resembles the definition of catachresis or even of trope more broadly, is especially suggestive of the linguistic abuses of Mrs. Brook's circle (slang, nicknames) that
so disconcert Longdon. Deflexion names an anacoluthic troping like the
turn or revolution characteristic of James's center of consciousness novels:
one thinks here of Burke's concept of deflection, associated with Freudian
displacement, and defined as "any slight bias or even unintended error
in our vocabulary for describing reality." (Paul de Man identifies Burkean
deflection with "the rhetorical basis of language.")[10] The original sense
of "awkward" contains a similar cluster of directional imagery: averted,
turned the wrong way, oblique, upside down, backward, perverse, not
in a straight direction. No less than the Jamesian reflector, the scenic
method proves susceptible to the awkwardness or "perversity" (another
etymological turn) of "appreciable, or more exactly . . . almost prepos-
terously appreciative, over-treatment." James's claim that the scenic
method yields a perfect narrative economy because "we are shut up
wholly to cross-relations" (*AN,* 114) echoes with the cross with which
he marks his recourse to the scenic method in the notebook entries on
The Ambassadors—a cross which, as noted above, refigures the very chiastic plot development it claims to evade. In each case, this crossing, turn,
or revolution names a version of the representational self-dismantling
intrinsic to the Jamesian reflector.

   The Awkward Age thus manifests an "unforeseen principle of growth"
that renders the novel a monstrous mutation from its germ. Like the
ironic center, the scenic method proves susceptible to an "accommodating irony" (*AN,* 98) or systematic displacement that counters its claims
to dramatic economy. This power of irony is aligned especially with
Nanda, the ironic outsider who alone in the novel possesses the capacity

   10.   De Man remarks, "Deflection is then conceived as a dialectical subversion of the
consistent link between sign and meaning that operates within grammatical patterns." See
Kenneth Burke, "Rhetoric—Old and New," in *New Rhetorics,* ed. Martin Steinmann, Jr.
(New York, 1967), 59–76, 75, and de Man, *Allegories of Reading,* 8.

for "expos[ing] everything and criticiz[ing]" (252). Thematically, the threat Nanda represents would appear antithetical to Maisie's missing moral sense; for whereas Maisie's ventriloquized consciousness produces the adulterous intrigues it observes, engendering a potentially endless narrative labyrinth, Nanda threatens to put an end to "talk," and to narrative discourse, altogether. Yet Nanda approximates Maisie's oxymoronic function as ironic center, for her irony unwittingly duplicates the vicious circle it would expose. As she declares of Longdon, "I set him off—what do you call it?—show him off: by his going round and round me as the acrobat on the horse, in the circus, goes round the clown" (247). She is a parodic vessel of consciousness, "a perfect fountain of curious knowledge" (354) or "a sort of little drain-pipe with everything flowing through" (260). As the inadvertent agent of awkwardness, Nanda must finally be excluded in the interest of Mrs. Brook's social, and James's representational, circle. Like Maisie, she undergoes a virtual or symbolic death, even as her final pairing with Longdon suggests a parodic marriage similar to the alliance between Maisie and Sir Claude hinted at and evaded in *What Maisie Knew.*[11] Her "arrangement," to use the novel's recurring term, permits the closure of James's own circle of representation. As Mitchy says of Nanda's effect on Tishy Grendon's circle, she makes it "compose" (116).

Nanda's compositional value is thematized by the novel's preoccupation with portraits and photographs, representational metaphors that give concrete form to her aestheticization. Both Aggie and Nanda are introduced by the photographs Longdon peruses, and the novel puns repeatedly on the photographic senses of "expose" and "develop." (In *The Art of the Novel,* James writes of the germ's transformative exposure in the "crucible of the imagination": "We here figure the morsel . . . not as boiled to nothing, but as exposed, in return for the taste it gives out, to

---

11. Several critics comment on the sexual implications of Nanda's ambiguous liaison with Longdon; see, for example, Edmund Wilson, *The Triple Thinkers: Twelve Essays on Literary Subjects* (New York, 1963), 128; Margaret Walters, " 'Keeping the Place Tidy for the Young Female Mind': *The Awkward Age,*" in *The Air of Reality,* ed. Goode, 196–218; and Silverman, who, however, sees Longdon as inscribed in a complex and triangulated relation with Van that ultimately reflects James's own "authorial phantasmatic" ("Too Early/Too Late: Subjectivity and the Primal Scene in Henry James," 169–70).

a new and richer saturation" [*AN,* 230]). What is exposed by Nanda's "retarded incorporation" (*AN,* 105) is not only her questionable moral sense but also her incorporation into a deathlike fixity akin to the funerary sculptures with which Isabel identifies at the end of *Portrait.* Kaja Silverman's concept of the "photo session" may be helpful here: as against Lacan's mirror stage, in which subjectivity is constructed through the incorporation of an external image, the photo session describes the subject's appropriation as an image through the gaze of the cultural Other.[12] James's preface speaks of the trap inherent to the act of drawing the delimiting circle of representation: "though the relations of a human figure or a social occurrence are what make such objects interesting, they also make them, to the same tune, difficult to isolate, to surround with the sharp black line, to frame in the square, the circle, the charming oval, that helps make any arrangement of objects to become a picture" (*AN,* 101). Like the representational trope of the portrait, the photograph's "expressive oval" (41) figures the continuity between Mrs. Brook's "home circle" (44) and the vicious circle of the representational law that both exposes Nanda and frames her. As James notes in the preface, "The better the talk prevailing in any circle, accordingly, the more organized, the more complete, the element of precaution and exclusion" (*AN,* 104).

Van's "impossible book" (244), the French novel whose circulation stages Nanda's definitive and fatal exposure,[13] thus figures *The Awkward Age* itself. Like Van's, James's book is indelibly inscribed by the impossibility imputed to Nanda; as she says to Longdon, "it's I who am the horrible impossible and who have covered everything else with my own impossibility" (380). For all its scenic consistency, the novel rehearses the demise of the reflective center in Nanda's verbal collapse: " 'Ah, but I don't [love Van]—please believe me when I assure you I *don't!*' she broke out. It burst from her, flaring up, in a queer quaver that ended in something queerer still—in her abrupt collapse, on the spot, into the nearest chair, where she choked with a torrent of tears" (379). Her final interview

12.   Kaja Silverman, *The Acoustic Mirror: The Female Voice in Psychoanalysis and Cinema* (Bloomington, Ind., 1988), 161–62.

13.   On this scene, see in particular Brooks, *The Melodramatic Imagination,* 164–65, and Silverman, "Too Early/Too Late: Subjectivity and the Primal Scene in Henry James," 167–68.

with Longdon rhymes formally as well as thematically with the closing scene of *What Maisie Knew*. Longdon recognizes the text's impasse, "the pass we've come to" (375): "What difference in the world does it make—what difference ever?"; "You don't know, you don't know!" he repeated"; "So it shows, so it shows—!" "Ah, Nanda, Nanda!" "It's I—it's I" (380). Nanda finally loses not only her standpoint or *locus standi* but her power of articulation, the very capacity for talk by which (unlike Maisie) she is defined. The stichomythic repetition that closes *The Awkward Age* uncannily replays the final pages of *What Maisie Knew*, leaving Nanda in a state of wordlessness or infancy (*infans*) that reinstates Maisie's irremediable dilemma. We seem to have come full circle, despite the text's stated intention of leaving behind the representational problematics of the central consciousness.

The "eternal English false position [ ]" (64) satirized by the novel names a representational as well as social conundrum, a false position like that of the center of consciousness itself. Despite the precautionary economy of the scenic method, *The Awkward Age* replicates the sacrificial dynamics of the center of consciousness. If there is a lesson to be learned from this unwitting replication, however, it eludes James, who laments in the preface that "nothing is wanting save, I confess, some grasp of its final lesson." Nevertheless, he speculates that such a lesson, if it could be grasped, would reveal the operative "law" behind it (*AN*, 100).

Whatever law of narrative may be illustrated by *The Awkward Age*, it cannot be named or identified, any more than the novel's germ and law, its origin and underlying principle. As Van muses of the law illustrated by the events witnessed in Mrs. Brook's circle, "It's the law—what is it?—the 'great law' of something or other" (356). It remains, as Mr. Longdon concludes of one of Nanda's conversational enigmas, a "conundrum" (174)—a puzzling question, enigmatical statement, or a thing that one is puzzled to name, a "what-d'ye-call it" (rare, *OED* 5). Sir Claude is equally at a loss to articulate the vicious circle of *What Maisie Knew*: "It's the same old vicious circle—and when I say vicious I don't mean a pun, a what-d'-ye-call-'em" (335). The lesson to be learned from either the center of consciousness or the scenic method may be a conundrum in this last sense, a puzzle unable to be grasped or formulated in language that does not repeat the terms of the conundrum itself.

My closing gesture here toward a disconcertment of James's principal representational categories is intended to dramatize the power and complexity of a representational praxis that cuts across such abstract distinctions. To argue that James's representational praxis is at odds with its own theory, or rather that both theory and praxis are internally incoherent, is not to impute to James a failure of conceptualization or narrative achievement, but to tease out the heterogeneous elements of his texts themselves, whether fictional or critical. This heterogeneity is a recurring subject of *The Art of the Novel,* which could itself be shown to play out a version of the rhetorical logic traced here. The enterprise of the critical prefaces in a sense posits a center of consciousness by postulating James's retrospective mastery and self-fashioning as reader of his own work. But as we have seen, such claims to mastery are always qualified or undone by the linguistic fabric of the prefaces themselves, whose enterprise James also terms "monstrous" (*AN,* 47). One small example of such qualification is the organization of the final three prefaces, which reverses the compositional priority of *The Ambassadors* and *The Wings of the Dove* (written after *The Ambassadors* but published before it), thus subtly putting in question the linear narrative of development, of "the continuity of an artist's endeavour, the growth of his whole operative consciousness" promised in the opening preface (*AN,* 4).

If the prefaces do not recapture an origin for James's fictions, neither do they announce the closure of a definitive understanding. Their task of "re-appropriation" leaves a remainder or residuum whose discharge remains permanently deferred by the conclusion of James's antepenultimate preface, that to *The Wings of the Dove:* "I become conscious of overstepping my space without having brought the full quantity to light. The failure leaves me with a burden of residuary comment of which I yet boldly hope elsewhere to discharge myself" (*AN,* 306). James's terminology of residue and residuum, familiar from *What Maisie Knew,* resonates suggestively with Shoshana Felman's reflection upon the textual residue inherent in reading: "The question of a reading's 'truth' must be at least complicated and re-thought through another question, which Freud, indeed, has raised, and taught us to articulate: what does such 'truth' (or any 'truth') leave out? What is it *made to miss?* What does it have as its function to overlook? What, precisely, is its residue, the *re-*

mainder it does not account for?"[14] The critical prefaces aspire to account for the essential unaccountability of the center of consciousness, even as they acknowledge the ultimate undecidability of whether their own interpretive insights have the status of a constative discovery or performative imposition of meaning—the two theories implied by James's incompatible figures for revision as a cleaning of the painter's canvas (an implicit figure of unveiling) or as an addition of new varnish, a retrospective projection of meaning (*AN,* 10–11). Like the novels read here, the critical prefaces themselves leave a residue that can neither be mastered nor squared—but this is a burden elsewhere to be discharged.

14.   Shoshana Felman, "Turning the Screw of Interpretation," in *Literature and Psychoanalysis: The Question of Reading: Otherwise,* ed. Felman (Baltimore, 1982), 94–207, 117.

Bibliography

Agnew, Jean-Christophe. "The Consuming Visions of Henry James." In *The Culture of Consumption: Critical Essays on American History 1880–1980*, edited by Richard Wightman Fox and T. Jackson Lears. New York, 1983.

Amorós, José Antonio Álvarez. "Henry James's 'Organic Form' and Classical Rhetoric." *Comparative Literature*, XLVI (1994), 40–64.

Anderson, Quentin. *The American Henry James*. New Brunswick, 1957.

Anesko, Michael. *"Friction with the Market": Henry James and the Profession of Authorship*. New York, 1986.

Arac, Jonathan. *Critical Genealogies: Historical Situations for Postmodern Literary Studies*. New York, 1987.

Armstrong, Paul. *The Phenomenology of Henry James*. Chapel Hill, 1983.

Auerbach, Jonathan. "Executing the Model: Painting, Sculpture and Romance-Writing in *The Marble Faun*." *English Literary History*, XLVII (1980), 103–20.

——. *The Romance of Failure: First-Person Fictions of Poe, Hawthorne, and James*. New York, 1989.

Badger, Reid. "The Character and Myth of Hyacinth: A Key to *The Princess Casamassima*." *Arizona Quarterly*, XXXII (1976), 316–26.

Banta, Martha. "Beyond Post-Modernism: The Sense of History in *The Princess Casamassima*." *Henry James Review*, III (1982), 96–107.

——. "The Quality of Experience in *What Maisie Knew*." *New England Quarterly*, XLII (1969), 483–510.

——, ed. *New Essays on "The American."* Cambridge, U.K., 1987.

Barnett, Louise K. "Speech in *The Ambassadors*: Woollett and Paris as Linguistic Communities." *Novel: A Forum on Fiction*, XVI (1983), 215–29.

Bell, Ian F. A. *Henry James and the Past: Readings into Time*. Houndmills, U.K., 1991.

————, ed. *Henry James: Fiction as History.* London, 1984.

Bell, Millicent. *Meaning in Henry James.* Cambridge, Mass., 1991.

Bercovitch, Sacvan. "The Revision of Rowland Mallet." *Nineteenth-Century Fiction,* XXIV (1969), 210–21.

Bersani, Leo. *A Future for Astyanax: Character and Desire in Literature.* New York, 1984.

————. "The Narrator as Center in *The Wings of the Dove.*" *Modern Fiction Studies,* VI (1960), 131–44.

Bewley, Marius. *The Complex Fate.* London, 1952.

Blackmur, R. P. *Studies in Henry James.* Edited by Veronica A. Makowsky. New York, 1983.

Blair, Sara. "Henry James and the Paradox of Literary Mastery." *Philosophy and Literature,* XV (1991), 89–102.

Blanchot, Maurice. *Le Livre à venir.* Paris, 1959.

Boone, Joseph. "Modernist Maneuverings in the Marriage Plot: Breaking Ideologies of Gender and Genre in James's *The Golden Bowl.*" *PMLA,* CI (1986), 374–88.

Bradbury, Nicola. *Henry James: The Later Novels.* Oxford, 1979.

————. " 'Nothing that is not there and the nothing that is': The Celebration of Absence in *The Wings of the Dove.*" In *Henry James: Fiction as History,* edited by Ian F. A. Bell. Houndmills, U.K., 1991.

Brodhead, Richard. *The School of Hawthorne.* New York, 1986.

Brooks, Peter. *The Melodramatic Imagination: Balzac, Henry James, Melodrama, and the Mode of Excess.* New Haven, 1976.

————. *Reading for the Plot: Design and Intention in Narrative.* New York, 1984.

Brown, Christopher. "The Rhetoric of Closure in *What Maisie Knew.*" *Style,* XX (1986), 58–65.

Brudney, Daniel. "Knowledge and Silence: *The Golden Bowl* and Moral Philosophy." *Critical Inquiry,* XVI (1990), 397–437.

Burke, Kenneth. *A Rhetoric of Motives.* 1950; rpr. Berkeley, 1969.

————. "Rhetoric—Old and New." In *New Rhetorics,* edited by Martin Steinmann, Jr. New York, 1967.

Cameron, Sharon. *Thinking in Henry James.* Chicago, 1989.

Cargill, Oscar. *The Novels of Henry James.* New York, 1961.

Carroll, David. *The Subject in Question: The Languages of Theory and the Strategies of Fiction.* Chicago, 1982.

Caserio, Robert L. *Plot, Story, and the Novel: From Dickens and Poe to the Modern Period.* Princeton, 1979.

Chase, Cynthia. *Decomposing Figures: Rhetorical Readings in the Romantic Tradition.* Baltimore, 1986.

Chatman, Seymour. *The Later Style of Henry James.* Oxford, 1972.

Cohan, Steven, and Linda M. Shires. *Telling Stories: A Theoretical Analysis of Narrative Fiction.* New York, 1988.

Cohen, Paula Marantz. *The Daughter's Dilemma: Family Process and the Nineteenth-Century Domestic Novel.* Ann Arbor, 1991.

Coleridge, Samuel Taylor. *Selected Poetry and Prose of Coleridge.* Edited by Donald A. Stauffer. New York, 1951.

Conn, Peter J. "*Roderick Hudson:* The Role of the Observer." *Nineteenth-Century Fiction,* XXVI (1971), 65–82.

Craig, David M. "The Indeterminacy of the End: Maggie Verver and the Limits of Imagination." *Henry James Review,* III (1982), 133–44.

Craig, Randall. " 'Read[ing] the unspoken into the spoken': Interpreting *What Maisie Knew.*" *Henry James Review,* II (1981), 204–12.

Cross, Mary. "The 'Drama of Discrimination': Style as Plot in *The Ambassadors.*" *Language and Style,* XVIII (1985), 46–63.

———. " 'To Find the Names': *The Ambassadors.*" *Papers on Language and Literature,* XIX (1983), 402–18.

Culler, Jonathan. *The Pursuit of Signs: Semiotics, Literature, Deconstruction.* Ithaca, 1981.

Culver, Stuart. "Censorship and Intimacy: Awkwardness in *The Awkward Age.*" *English Literary History,* XLVIII (1981), 368–86.

Davis, Lloyd. *Sexuality and Textuality in Henry James: Reading Through the Virginal.* New York, 1988.

De Man, Paul. *Allegories of Reading: Figural Language in Rousseau, Nietzsche, Rilke, and Proust.* New Haven, 1979.

———. *Blindness and Insight: Essays in the Rhetoric of Contemporary Criticism.* Rev. ed. Minneapolis, 1983.

———. *The Resistance to Theory.* Minneapolis, 1986.

Derrida, Jacques. *Writing and Difference.* Translated by Alan Bass. Chicago, 1978.

Dryden, Edgar A. *The Form of American Romance.* Baltimore, 1988.

Dupee, F. W., ed. *The Question of Henry James.* New York, 1945.

Eagleton, Terry. *Criticism and Ideology: A Study in Marxist Literary Theory.* 1976; London, 1988.

Eckstein, Barbara. "Unsquaring the Squared Route of *What Maisie Knew.*" *Henry James Review,* IX (1988), 177–87.

Edel, Leon. *Henry James: A Life.* New York, 1985.

Esch, Deborah. "Promissory Notes: The Prescription of the Future in *The Princess Casamassima.*" *American Literary History,* I (1989), 317–38.

———. " 'Understanding Allegories': Reading *The Portrait of a Lady.*" In *Henry James's "The Portrait of a Lady,"* edited by Harold Bloom. New York, 1987.

Faber, M. D. "Henry James: Revolutionary Involvement, the Princess, and the Hero." *American Imago,* XXXVII (1980), 245–77.

Feidelson, Charles. "James and the 'Man of Imagination.' " *Literary Theory and Structure: Essays in Honor of William K. Wimsatt,* edited by Frank Brady, John Palmer, and Martin Price. New Haven, 1973.

Felman, Shoshana. "Turning the Screw of Interpretation." In *Literature and Psychoanalysis: The Question of Reading: Otherwise,* edited by Shoshana Felman. Baltimore, 1982.

Fischer, Mike. "The Jamesian Revolution in *The Princess Casamassima:* A Lesson in Bookbinding." *Henry James Review,* IX (1988), 87–104.

Fletcher, Angus. *Allegory: The Theory of a Symbolic Mode.* 1964; Ithaca, 1982.

Fogel, Daniel Mark. *Henry James and the Structure of the Romantic Imagination.* Baton Rouge, 1981.

Foster, Dennis. "Maisie Supposed to Know: Amo(u)ral Analysis." *Henry James Review,* V (1984), 207–16.

Fowler, Virginia C. "Milly Theale's Malady of Self." *Novel: A Forum on Fiction,* XIV (1980), 57–74.

Freedman, Jonathan. *Professions of Taste: Henry James, British Aestheticism, and Commodity Culture.* Stanford, 1990.

Freud, Sigmund. *The Standard Edition of the Complete Psychological Works of Sigmund Freud.* Translated by James Strachey. 24 vols. London, 1953–74.

Galbraith, Mary. "What Everybody Knew Versus What Maisie Knew: The Change in Epistemological Perspective from the Prologue to the Opening of Chapter 1 in *What Maisie Knew.*" *Style,* XXIII (1989), 197–212.

Gelley, Alexander. *Narrative Crossings: Theory and Pragmatics of Prose Fiction.* Baltimore, 1987.

Girard, René. *Deceit, Desire, and the Novel: Self and Other in Literary Structure.* Translated by Yvonne Freccero. Baltimore, 1965.

Goetz, William. *Henry James and the Darkest Abyss of Romance.* Baton Rouge, 1986.

Goode, John, ed. *The Air of Reality: New Essays on Henry James.* London, 1972.

Graham, Kenneth. *Henry James: The Drama of Fulfilment.* Oxford, 1975.

Greenslade, William. "The Power of Advertising: Chad Newsome and the Meaning of Paris in *The Ambassadors.*" *English Literary History,* XLIX (1982), 99–122.

Greenwald, Elissa. " 'I and the Abyss': Transcendental Romance in *The Wings of the Dove.*" *Studies in the Novel,* XVIII (1986), 177–92.

Gribble, Jennifer. "Value in *The Golden Bowl.*" *Critical Review,* XXVII (1985), 50–65.

Griffin, Susan M. *The Historical Eye: The Texture of the Visual in Late James.* Boston, 1991.

Hartman, Geoffrey H. *Beyond Formalism.* New Haven, 1970.

Hawthorne, Nathaniel. *The Marble Faun.* New York, 1961.

————. *Mosses from an Old Manse.* Columbus, Ohio, 1974. Vol. X of *The Centenary Edition of the Works of Nathaniel Hawthorne.* 20 vols.

Hay, Eloise Knapp. "Proust, James, Conrad, and Impressionism." *Style,* XXII (1988), 368–81.

Hertz, Neil. *The End of the Line: Essays on Psychoanalysis and the Sublime.* New York, 1985.

Higgins, Joanna A. "The Ambassadorial Motif in *The Ambassadors.*" *Journal of Narrative Technique,* VIII (1978), 165–75.

Hocks, Richard A. *Henry James and Pragmatistic Thought: A Study in the Relationship Between the Philosophy of William James and the Literary Art of Henry James.* Chapel Hill, 1974.

Holland, Laurence Bedwell. *The Expense of Vision: Essays on the Craft of Henry James.* 1964; rpr. Baltimore, 1982.

Hoople, Robin F. "Iconological Characterization in James's *The Ambassadors.*" *American Literature,* LX (1988), 416–32.

Horne, Philip. *Henry James and Revision: The New York Edition.* Oxford, 1990.

Howe, Irving. *Politics and the Novel.* New York, 1957.

Ian, Marcia. "Consecrated Diplomacy and the Concretion of Self." *Henry James Review,* VII (1985), 27–33.

————. "The Elaboration of Privacy in *The Wings of the Dove.*" *English Literary History,* LI (1984), 107–36.

Isle, Walter. *Experiments in Form: Henry James's Novels, 1896–1901.* Cambridge, Mass., 1968.

James, Henry. *The Ambassadors.* Edited by Christopher Butler. 1903; Oxford, 1985.

————. *The Art of the Novel.* Edited by R. P. Blackmur. 1934; Boston, 1984.

————. *The Awkward Age.* 1899; New York, 1981.

————. *The Complete Notebooks of Henry James.* Edited by Leon Edel and Lyall H. Powers. New York, 1987.

————. *The Golden Bowl.* 1904; rpr. Harmondsworth, U.K., 1966.

————. *"In the Cage" and Other Stories.* Edited by S. Gorley Putt. London, 1972.

————. *Literary Criticism: Essays on Literature, American Writers, English Writers.* New York, 1984.

————. *Literary Criticism: French Writers, Other European Writers, Prefaces to the New York Edition.* New York, 1984.

————. *Novels 1871–1880*. New York, 1983.

————. *The Novels and Tales of Henry James,* The New York Edition. 26 vols. 1907–17; rpr. New York, 1935–45.

————. *The Portrait of a Lady.* Edited by Nicola Bradbury. 1881; Oxford, 1985.

————. *Roderick Hudson.* 1875; Oxford, 1980.

————. *The Sacred Fount.* 1901; New York, 1953.

————. *"The Turn of the Screw" and Other Short Fiction.* Toronto, 1981.

————. *The Wings of the Dove.* 1902; New York, 1965.

Jay, Gregory S. *America the Scrivener: Deconstruction and the Subject of Literary History.* Ithaca, 1990.

Jeffers, Thomas L. "Maisie's Moral Sense: Finding Out for Herself." *Nineteenth-Century Fiction,* XXXIV (1979), 154–72.

Kairschner, Mimi. "The Traces of Capitalist Patriarchy in the Silences of *The Golden Bowl.*" *Henry James Review,* V (1984), 187–92.

Kaplan, Fred. *Henry James: The Imagination of Genius: A Biography.* New York, 1992.

Kappeler, Susanne. *Writing and Reading in Henry James.* New York, 1980.

Kaston, Carren. *Imagination and Desire in the Novels of Henry James.* New Brunswick, 1984.

Komar, Kathleen L. "Language and Character Delineation in *The Wings of the Dove.*" *Twentieth-Century Literature,* XXIX (1983), 471–87.

Krook, Dorothea. *The Ordeal of Consciousness in Henry James.* Cambridge, U.K., 1962.

Lebowitz, Naomi. *The Imagination of Loving: Henry James's Legacy to the Novel.* Detroit, 1965.

Levenson, Michael. *Modernism and the Fate of Individuality: Character and Novelistic Form from Conrad to Woolf.* Cambridge, U.K., 1991.

Locke, John. *An Essay Concerning Human Understanding.* Edited by Alexander Campbell Fraser. 2 vols. New York, 1959.

Lodge, David. *The Language of Fiction: Essays in Criticism and Verbal Analysis of the English Novel.* New York, 1966.

Lohn, Linda. " 'An Abyss of Abysses': Will, Morality, and Artistic Imagination in James's *Roderick Hudson.*" *Henry James Review,* XII (1991), 93–100.

Lubbock, Percy. *The Craft of Fiction.* 1921; rpr. New York, 1957.

Lukacher, Ned. *Primal Scenes: Literature, Philosophy, Psychoanalysis.* Ithaca, 1986.

Marotta, Kenny. "*What Maisie Knew:* The Question of Our Speech." *English Literary History,* XLVI (1979), 495–508.

Marovitz, Sanford E. "*Roderick Hudson:* James's *Marble Faun.*" *Texas Studies in Literature and Language,* XI (1970), 1427–43.

Matthiessen, F. O. *American Renaissance: Art and Expression in the Age of Emerson and Whitman*. 1941; rpr. New York, 1968.

———. *Henry James: The Major Phase*. London, 1946.

McCormack, Peggy. "Exchange Economy in Henry James's *The Awkward Age*." *University of Mississippi Studies in English*, V (1984), 182–202.

———. "The Semiotics of Economic Language in James's Fiction." *American Literature*, LVIII (1986), 540–56.

McWhirter, David. *Desire and Love in Henry James: A Study of the Late Novels*. Cambridge, U.K., 1989.

Miller, D. A. *Narrative and Its Discontents: Problems of Closure in the Traditional Novel*. Princeton, 1981.

Miller, J. Hillis. "Ariachne's Broken Woof." *Georgia Review*, XXXI (1977), 44–60.

———. "Ariadne's Thread: Repetition and the Narrative Line." *Critical Inquiry*, III (1976), 57–77.

———. *The Ethics of Reading*. New York, 1987.

———. *Fiction and Repetition: Seven English Novels*. Cambridge, Mass., 1982.

———. "The Figure in the Carpet." *Poetics Today*, I (1980), 107–18.

———. *Hawthorne and History*. Cambridge, Mass., 1991.

———. *Illustration*. Cambridge, Mass., 1992.

———. "Is There an Ethics of Reading?" In *Reading Narrative: Form, Ethics, Ideology*, edited by James Phelan. Columbus, Ohio, 1989.

———. "Narrative and History." *English Literary History*, XLI (1974), 455–73.

———. *Versions of Pygmalion*. Cambridge, Mass., 1990.

Mitchell, Lee Clark. "The Sustaining Duplicities of *The Wings of the Dove*." *Texas Studies in Literature and Language*, XXIX (1987), 187–214.

Mizruchi, Susan L. *The Power of Historical Knowledge: Narrating the Past in Hawthorne, James, and Dreiser*. Princeton, 1988.

———. "Reproducing Women in *The Awkward Age*." *Representations*, XXXVIII (1992), 101–30.

Moon, Michael. "Sexuality and Visual Terrorism in *The Wings of the Dove*." *Criticism*, XXVIII (1986), 427–43.

Mull, Donald L. *Henry James's "Sublime Economy": Money as Symbolic Center in the Fiction*. Middletown, Conn., 1973.

Nettels, Elsa. "Action and Point of View in *Roderick Hudson*." *English Studies*, LIII (1972), 238–47.

Norrman, Ralf. *The Insecure World of Henry James's Fiction: Intensity and Ambiguity*. London, 1982.

Novak, Barbara. *American Painting of the Nineteenth Century: Realism, Idealism, and the American Experience.* 2nd ed. New York, 1979.

Nussbaum, Martha Craven. " 'Finely Aware and Richly Responsible': Literature and the Moral Imagination." *Literature and the Question of Philosophy,* edited by Anthony J. Cascardi. Baltimore, 1987.

————. "Flawed Crystals: James's *The Golden Bowl* and Literature as Moral Philosophy." *New Literary History,* XV (1983), 25–50.

Oerlemans, Onno. "Literary Value and *The Wings of the Dove.*" *English Studies in Canada,* XVII (1991), 177–96.

Person, Leland, "Strether's 'Penal Form': The Pleasure of Imaginative Surrender." *Papers on Language and Literature,* XXIII (1987), 27–40.

Perosa, Sergio. *Henry James and the Experimental Novel.* Charlottesville, 1978.

Poirier, Richard. *The Comic Sense of Henry James.* New York, 1967.

————. *A World Elsewhere: The Place of Style in American Literature.* 1966; rpr. Madison, Wis., 1985.

Porte, Joel, ed. *New Essays on "The Portrait of a Lady."* Cambridge, U.K., 1990.

Porter, Carolyn. "History and Literature: 'After the New Historicism.' " *New Literary History,* XXI (1990), 253–72.

————. *Seeing and Being: The Plight of the Participant Observer in Emerson, James, Adams, and Faulkner.* Middletown, Conn., 1981.

Poulet, Georges. *The Metamorphoses of the Circle.* Translated by Carley Dawson and Elliott Coleman. Baltimore, 1966.

Powers, Lyall. *Henry James and the Naturalist Movement.* East Lansing, Mich., 1971.

Przybylowicz, Donna. *Desire and Repression: The Dialectic of Self and Other in the Late Works of Henry James.* Tuscaloosa, 1986.

Raphael, Linda. "Levels of Knowing: Development of Consciousness in *The Wings of the Dove.*" *Henry James Review,* XI (1990), 58–71.

Reaney, Percy H. *A Dictionary of British Surnames.* London, 1958.

Reynolds, Mark. "Counting the Costs: The Infirmity of Art and *The Golden Bowl.*" *Henry James Review,* VI (1984), 15–25.

Rivkin, Julie. "The Logic of Delegation in *The Ambassadors.*" *PMLA,* CI (1986), 819–31.

————. "Resisting Readers and Reading Effects: Some Speculations on Reading and Gender." In *Narrative Poetics: Innovations, Limits, Challenges,* edited by James Phelan. Columbus, 1987.

Ron, Moshe. "The Art of the Portrait According to James." *Yale French Studies,* LXIX (1985), 222–37.

Rothfield, Lawrence. *Vital Signs: Medical Realism in Nineteenth-Century Fiction.* Princeton, 1992.

Rowe, John Carlos. *Henry Adams and Henry James: The Emergence of a Modern Consciousness*. Ithaca, 1976.

————. *The Theoretical Dimensions of Henry James*. Madison, Wis., 1984.

————. *Through the Custom-House: Nineteenth-Century American Fiction and Modern Theory*. Baltimore, 1982.

Sabin, Margery. *The Dialect of the Tribe: Speech and Community in Modern Fiction*. New York, 1987.

Salmon, Richard. "The Secret of the Spectacle: Epistemology and Commodity Display in *The Ambassadors*." *Henry James Review*, XIV (1993), 43–54.

Scanlon, Margaret. "Terrorism and the Realistic Novel: Henry James and *The Princess Casamassima*." *Texas Studies in Literature and Language*, XXXIV (1992), 380–402.

Schirmeister, Pamela. *The Consolations of Space: The Place of Romance in Hawthorne, Melville, and James*. Stanford, 1990.

Schneider, Daniel J. *The Crystal Cage: Adventures of the Imagination in the Fiction of Henry James*. Lawrence, 1978.

Sears, Sallie. *The Negative Imagination: Form and Perspective in the Novels of Henry James*. Ithaca, 1968.

Sedgwick, Eve Kosofsky. *Between Men: English Literature and Male Homosocial Desire*. New York, 1985.

————. *Tendencies*. Durham, N.C., 1993.

Segal, Ora. *The Lucid Reflector: The Observer in Henry James's Fiction*. New Haven, 1969.

Seidel, Michael. *Exile and the Narrative Imagination*. New Haven, 1986.

Seltzer, Mark. *Henry James and the Art of Power*. Ithaca, 1984.

Silverman, Kaja. *The Acoustic Mirror: The Female Voice in Psychoanalysis and Cinema*. Bloomington, Ind., 1988.

————. "Too Early/Too Late: Subjectivity and the Primal Scene in Henry James." *Novel: A Forum on Fiction*, XXI (1988), 147–73.

Sklenicka, Carol J. "Henry James's Evasion of Ending in *The Golden Bowl*." *Henry James Review*, IV (1982), 50–60.

Steele, Meili. "The Drama of Reference in James's *The Golden Bowl*." *Novel: A Forum on Fiction*, XXI (1987), 73–88.

————. "Value and Subjectivity: The Dynamics of the Sentence in James's *The Ambassadors*." *Comparative Literature*, XLIII (1991), 113–33.

Stevens, Hugh. "Sexuality and the Aesthetic in *The Golden Bowl*." *Henry James Review*, XIV (1993), 55–71.

Stoehr, Taylor. "Words and Deeds in *The Princess Casamassima*." *English Literary History*, XXXVII (1970), 95–135.

Sussman, Henry. *The Hegelian Aftermath: Readings in Hegel, Kierkegaard, Freud, Proust, and James.* Baltimore, 1982.

Sypher, Eileen. "Anarchism and Gender: James's *The Princess Casamassima* and Conrad's *The Secret Agent*." *Henry James Review,* IX (1988), 1–16.

Tanner, Tony. *Scenes of Nature, Signs of Men.* Cambridge, U.K., 1987.

Tinter, Adeline. "*Roderick Hudson:* A Centennial Reading." *Henry James Review,* II (1981), 172–98.

Todorov, Tzvetan. *The Poetics of Prose.* Translated by Richard Howard. Ithaca, 1977.

———. "The Verbal Age." Translated by Patricia Martin Gibby. *Critical Inquiry,* IV (1977), 351–71.

Torgovnick, Marianna. *Closure in the Novel.* Princeton, 1981.

———. *The Visual Arts, Pictorialism, and the Novel: James, Lawrence, and Woolf.* Princeton, 1985.

Torsney, Cheryl B. "Specula(riza)tion in *The Golden Bowl*." *Henry James Review,* XII (1991), 141–46.

Trilling, Lionel. *The Liberal Imagination.* New York, 1953.

Turgenev, Ivan. *On the Eve.* Translated by Constance Garnett. London, 1973.

———. *Virgin Soil.* Translated by Constance Garnett. New York, 1920.

Walton, Priscilla L. *The Disruption of the Feminine in Henry James.* Toronto, 1992.

Ward, J. A. *The Imagination of Disaster: Evil in the Fiction of Henry James.* Lincoln, 1961.

———. *The Search for Form: Studies in the Structure of James's Fiction.* Chapel Hill, 1967.

Watt, Ian. "The First Paragraph of *The Ambassadors:* An Explication." *The Ambassadors.* Edited by S. P. Rosenbaum. New York, 1964.

Weinstein, Philip M. *Henry James and the Requirements of the Imagination.* Cambridge, Mass., 1971.

Weisbuch, Robert. *Atlantic Double-Cross: American Literature and British Influence in the Age of Emerson.* Chicago, 1986.

Welsh, Alexander. *Strong Representations: Narrative and Circumstantial Evidence in England.* Baltimore, 1992.

Weltzien, O. Alan. "The Seeds of James's Grand Monument, or When Growing Becomes Building." *Henry James Review,* XII (1991), 255–70.

Wicke, Jennifer A. *Advertising Fictions: Literature, Advertisement, and Social Reading.* New York, 1988.

Wilkinson, Myler. "Henry James and the Ethical Moment." *Henry James Review,* XI (1990), 153–75.

Williams, Merle A. *Henry James and the Philosophical Novel: Seeing and Being.* Cambridge, U.K., 1993.

Wilson, Edmund. *The Triple Thinkers: Twelve Essays on Literary Subjects.* New York, 1963.

Winner, Viola Hopkins. *Henry James and the Visual Arts.* Charlottesville, 1970.

Wolk, Merla. "Narration and Nurture in *What Maisie Knew.*" *Henry James Review,* IV (1983), 196–206.

Wutz, Michael. "The Word and the Self in *The Ambassadors.*" *Style,* XXV (1991), 89–103.

Yeazell, Ruth Barnard. *Language and Knowledge in the Late Novels of Henry James.* Chicago, 1971.

Young, Arlene. "Hypothetical Discourse as Ficelle in *The Golden Bowl.*" *American Literature,* LXI (1989), 382–97.

Zacharias, Greg. "James's Morality in *Roderick Hudson.*" *Henry James Review,* XI (1990), 115–32.

———. "The Language of Light and Dark and James's Moral Argument in *The Golden Bowl.*" *Papers on Language and Literature,* XXVI (1990), 249–70.

Ziarek, Ewa. " 'Surface Stratified on Surface': A Reading of Ahab's Allegory." *Criticism,* XXXI (1989), 271–86.

Zwinger, Lynda. *Daughters, Fathers, and the Novel: The Sentimental Romance of Heterosexuality.* Madison, Wis., 1991.

Index

Map The Crit

I
[
1) formal anal of [x] Goebz, Teahan ⎤ combine
                                       Hab, (y) ⎦

2) vs   anal
]

1) celebratory: linguistic/modernistic/[Nietzsche

II   ↳ vs Nietzsche
where sense 2) [I] ycc: deeply conservative   more approx: Schop
of art?

marking out a

part kind of text
1) signs → signs
2) self-reflexive dimension
   (often contained: allegory of reading)